D0561555

CONCILIUM
Religion in the Seventies

CONCILIUM

EDITORIAL DIRECTORS

Giuseppe Alberigo	Bologna	Italy
William Bassett	San Francisco	U.S.A.
Gregory Baum	Toronto	Canada
Franz Böckle	Bonn, Röttgen	West Germany
Antoine van den Boogaard	Nijmegen	Netherlands
Paul Brand	Ankeveen	Netherlands
Marie-Dominique Chenu O.P. (adviser)	Paris	France
Yves Congar O.P. (adviser)	Paris	France
Mariasusai Dhavamony S.J. (adviser)	Rome	Italy
Christian Duquoc O.P.	Lyon	France
Casiano Floristán	Madrid	Spain
Claude Geffré O.P.	Paris	France
Andrew Greeley	Chicago	U.S.A.
Norbert Greinacher	Tübingen	West Germany
Gustavo Gutiérrez Merino (adviser)	Lima	Peru
Peter Huizing S.J.	Nijmegen	Netherlands
Bas van Iersel S.M.M.	Nijmegen	Netherlands
Jean-Pierre Jossua O.P.	Paris	France
Hans Küng	Tübingen	West Germany
René Laurentin (adviser)	Paris	France
Luis Maldonado	Madrid	Spain
Johannes Baptist Metz	Münster	West Germany
Jürgen Moltmann	Tübingen	West Germany
Alois Müller	Lucerne	Switzerland
Roland Murphy O. CARM.	Durham, N.C.	U.S.A.
Jacques-Marie Pohier O.P.	Paris	France
David Power O.M.I.	Rome	Italy
Karl Rahner S.J. (adviser)	Munich	West Germany
Luigi Sartori (adviser)	Padua	Italy
Edward Schillebeeckx O.P.	Nijmegen	Netherlands
Herman Schmidt S.J.	Rome	Italy
David Tracy (adviser)	Chicago	U.S.A.
Anton Weiler	Nijmegen	Netherlands

LAY SPECIALIST ADVISERS

José Luis Aranguren	Madrid/Santa Barbara, Ca.	Spain/U.S.A.
Luciano Caglioti	Rome	Italy
August Wilhelm von Eiff	Bonn	West Germany
Paolo Freire	Geneva	Switzerland
André Hellegers	Washington, D.C.	U.S.A.
Barbara Ward Jackson	New York	U.S.A.
Harald Weinrich	Köln	West Germany

Concilium 2, 1977: Liturgy

GRACE LIBRARY, CARLOW COLLEGE
PITTSBURGH, PA. 15213

LITURGY AND CULTURAL RELIGIOUS TRADITIONS

Edited by
Herman Schmidt and David Power

BQ
371
C74
V.102

A CROSSROAD BOOK
The Seabury Press • New York

CATALOGUED

1977
The Seabury Press
815 Second Avenue
New York, N.Y. 10017

Copyright © 1977 by Stichting Concilium and The Seabury Press, Inc. All rights reserved. Nothing contained in this publication shall be multiplied and/or made public by
means of print, photographic print, microfilm, or in any other manner without the previous written consent of the Stichting Concilium, Nijmegen (Holland) and of The
Seabury Press, Inc., New York.

Library of Congress Catalog Card Number: 77-7847
ISBN: 0-8164-2146-3
Printed in the United States of America

CONTENTS

Editorial

POPULAR forms of religious expression, often somewhat at variance with liturgies, are a frequent subject of discussion. The topic is vast and often ambiguous. The terms used are hard to define, the extent and pluriformity of the phenomenon defies determination and accurate investigation. It is also difficult to say when there is evidence of superstition or sentiment, and when an authentic expression of faith.

In this issue of *Concilium* it is not our ambition to cover the whole ground. We try rather to concentrate on one point which pertains to the discussion. On the understanding that it is the intention of a religious system to give adequate and accessible expression to a people's quest for meaning, we have chosen to treat of the meeting between varying cultural traditions of religious significance. Clifford Geertz, an American anthropologist, speaks of religion as a cultural system in which all aspects of human life are interrelated in a meaningful way.[1] Perhaps Geertz's description of a religious system applies less easily to Christianity or to other religions with missionary traditions than to religions which appear more readily to be native to a given people. With missionary religions, the first proclamation is in many ways opposed to existing cultural traditions. What can happen is that the 'official' religious expression is not adequate or easily accessible to many people, so that they continue to inhabit other forms or seek to merge the old and the new. A contrast between official liturgies and other forms of religious expression may not be an ideal, but it is a fact of history and of present reality which needs examination. It may have something to do with the failure of liturgies to express a cultural mood

1

in a truly comprehensive and accessible way.

Prescinding from the question of how the earliest Christian ritual came into being, for later eras we could probably trace a pattern of development:

    (a) an existing religious expression is supplemented by an extraneous element which often tries to replace it;

    (b) from the meeting of these forms there results either a merging of forms, or the coexistence of contrasting and at times diverging forms.

Given this situation, there are three points in particular which we have in mind for this number of *Concilium*:

    (a) The encounter between ancient and new forms of religious expression, when the new comes from a source external to a people.

    (b) The development of religious expression which merges Christian and non-Christian forms; an expression which may enjoy popularity among an entire people or may be found only in a certain section, even perhaps an élite.

    (c) The development of religious expression in such a way that it stands for the cultural values and aspirations of a given people.

The first section of the issue will take some examples from history which show concretely how cultural meaning and religious expression intertwine. The second section touches on questions of more immediate present-day interest. These two sections are followed by a theological conclusion, written by one of the editors. Finally, in a bulletin we take the example of how the question of *religiosidad popular* is treated in Spain in current studies. This will help to put the articles in this review into a broader context. We thought that the example of one country would be more helpful than a broad survey of many countries or continents.   HERMAN SCHMIDT

Notes

1. C. Geertz, 'Religion as a Cultural System', in M. Banton, *Anthropological Approaches to the Study of Religion* (London, 1966), pp. 1–46.

Jacques Fontaine

The Meeting of Cultures in Hispanic Iconography from the Fourth to the Seventh Century

THE evangelization of Roman Spain was already far advanced in the mid-third century whence the first dated documents on the subject have come down to us. In 254 we encounter, in the correspondence of Cyprian of Carthage, the complaints recorded by the communities of Merida, Leon and Astorga against their pastors who had apostasized but refused to give up their sees. In 259, during the persecution of Valerian, Bishop of Tarragona Fructuosa mounted the scaffold with his two deacons, Augurious and Eulogius. The *Acts* of their martyr-dom are among the most authentic. These extremely ancient documents allow me to pinpoint my subject.

  They indicate first that Christianity had not only taken root in the most Romanized coastal regions but that it was no less firmly established in Lusitania, and even in the distant cities in the north-west of the peninsula, in those provinces most recently conquered and sub-dued by Rome. In those essentially Celtic regions, the indigenous cultures were not Romanized so early or so completely as in the valleys of the Ebro and the Guadalquivir, the latter having been from 197 B.C. the Roman provinces of near and further Spain.

  The result is that the indigenous religions, in spite of a Latinization testified to by the inscriptions on funeral monuments, enjoyed a stability—not to say revival—in those regions, under the liberal political tutelage of the Roman Empire. For this reason I shall pay special attention to this 'north-western quarter' of the peninsula where, in any case, the most interesting remains of seventh-century Visigothic sculpture are preserved.

In their letter of 254, the community of Merida complained that their apostate bishop had scandalized them on an earlier occasion by having the deceased members of his family buried with pagans in a cemetery belonging to a *collegium*. Now these *collegia* are known to have been professional associations of, for the most part, less affluent citizens and in particular artisans. This bishop, therefore, probably came from the lower echelons of the social hierarchy of his city. Half a century later, on the other hand, the city of Elvira (near present-day Granada) questioned the way in which certain Christians functioned as magistrates, or in the pagan priesthood, as well as the abuses committed by certain landowners (who we know, moreover, more often than not possessed a residence in town). All this suggests that one should think in terms not of social opposition (rich pagans and poor Christians) but rather of a geopolitical and cultural antithesis between town and country, if one is to get the problems of the meeting of cultures in Hispanic Christianity into perspective, particularly in the north-west where the country districts were evangelized later and more slowly than elsewhere. Martin of Braga's celebrated sermon *De correctione rusticorum* reveals the surprising vitality of rural paganism in these regions even at the end of the sixth century.

The cultural expression of Christianity, as observed in the forms of religious iconography, was subsequently to go through a process of evolution linked with that of Roman civilization and the indigenous cultures. Established first in the towns—principal centres of the language and culture of Rome—Christianity very soon appeared as an eastern religion in Latin dress. Its hierarchy, moreover, was distributed among the readymade zones formed by the cities. The result was that Christianization and Romanization went increasingly hand in hand, especially when Christianity was recognized by Roman law (313) and then became the state religion (380). What is more, the proclamation of the Word of God—translated into Latin from the second century onwards—could only be understood there by a Latin-speaking, if not completely Romanized, audience. That is why the evangelization of the country districts was to be a decisive factor in the definitive Latinization of the West. In Spain itself only the Basque region was to survive that process.

These three preliminary sections have set the scene and presented the factors involved in the dialectical evolution I am trying to trace. On the one hand, in Hispania, the indigenous paganism possessed very vigorous traditions, the iconographic expression of which has been preserved for us in the funerary monuments usually known as 'Hispano-Roman steles'. Confronted with this sacred art, Christianity was expressed at first in a cultural and iconographical mode of expression imported (in all senses of the word) from Rome, and reserved for a privileged élite, at least as far as funeral sculpture was concerned—the only early Christian art of which we have Spanish examples that are still iconographically important. It was only after the fall of Rome in the fifth century, during the rule of the Visigoths (late sixth and seventh centuries) that the evangelization of the north-west really progressed, in spite of the still vigorous resistance of rural paganism; then some degree of synthesis of religious iconographies became possible and even necessary. The best examples of this synthesis of Roman, indigenous and oriental themes are preserved in the decoration of the small churches in the north.

FUNERAL TRADITIONS

From the Celtic area of north and north-western Spain a rich collection of funeral steles has come down to us which displays a religious iconography at once homogeneous in its themes and diverse in regional forms and techniques. The majority of the pieces date from the late Empire (second to third centuries). Not only the earlier traces of Hispano-Roman art but its newer manifestations survived the Edict of Milan and the century of the Christian Empire: in the Cantabrian Pyrenees a dedication to a local god was discovered recently, dated 399—nearly twenty years after the Edict of Thessalonica of 380. We must therefore assume that the production of the Hispano-Roman steles took place alongside the importation or production of the paleo-Christian sarcophagi of the fourth and fifth centuries. In the less Romanized regions, the same workshops sometimes provided pieces with a distinctive iconography, according to the religious convictions of their clients. Hence we find among the products of the workshop of La Bureba (the Briviesca region north-east of Burgos) a form of coexistence analogous to that still to be found in Rome in the second half of the fourth century, in the cubicles with their Christian or pagan iconography, at the hypogeum of the Via Latina.

The iconography of these northern funeral steles is essentially religious, whether it is a question of scenes with human figures, representations of plants, the signs of the zodiac, or architectural patterns. Unlike that of Gant, it offers hardly any realistic representations of scenes from the everyday life of the dead. More primitive in overall execution, it is also more abstract, and more mysterious inasmuch as it is more authentically sacred. It sets out, primarily, to represent in a figurative or above all symbolic way the life of the departed beyond the grave and the transcendence of the divine universe that he has entered by way of death. The regional variations in these figurative representations reflect the complex ethnic differences in the northern *meseta*. There the waves of Indo-European invaders came up against either the last traces of prehistoric populations who had mostly taken refuge in the Pyrenees, or the expansion of Iberian peoples and civilizations as they made their way from the Mediterranean regions to the *mesetas*. Hence the brilliance of the so-called Celto-Iberian points of contact on both sides of the valley of the upper Tage and in the region of the upper Duero.

We can pass quickly over the heroic representations of the dead as warrior horsemen or huntsmen, as they were to have little or no future in the synthetic iconography of the Visigothic period (though a few traces of them are to be found in curious figures on the inner friezes of the apse of San Pedro at Nava). Greater attention must be given to the representations of animals and plants (birds and rabbits; classic Mediterranean décor of the vine with foliated scrolls and bunches of grapes, the latter most probably preserving its Dionysian overtones of immortality. More interesting still, given the religious and aesthetic uses to which they were to be put in seventh-century art, are the images of the heavenly bodies: the sun and the moon in the form of circles, rosettes, swastikas and crescents. The celestial representations found on certain Portuguese megaliths reveal the ancient Hispanic bases of the beliefs connected with them which were reinforced under the Empire by the considerable penetration of eastern religions into those regions. They were to continue in syncretist, hardly Christianized forms in the Priscillianist heresy in fifth- and sixth-century Galicia; and the rise of sun-worship in the Empire in the third century can only have helped to ensure their transmission, even then, to the peninsula of the Lower Byzantine Empire.

Finally, special mention must be made of what some authors have described as images of the gates of hell on the steles. Double or triple, and often occupying the base of the stele, these are semicircular blind arches or horseshoe arches. The rich development of the arch in Christian Visigothic and later Mozarabic architecture makes one look with redoubled interest at these patterns. Do they show the entrance into the world beyond through which one passes at death? Are they merely imitations of actual earthly mausoleums? Are they symbolic creations of the religious imagination or purely monumental decoration intended to give a touch of solemnity? These hypotheses are not mutually exclusive, and the properly religious significance (rite of passage through death which transcends life) remains the most profound.

At the same time the problem of further transmission is reversed. Longitudinal arches—or even transverse arches, like the trio of extended arches separating the nave from the sanctuary in such Mozarabic basilicas as Escalada (tenth-century but a Visigothic legacy, as Schlunk's study of Sao Giao of Nazare has shown)—are seen in a new light as a result; the natural religion of the life beyond could help to clarify here the Christian use of secular symbolism.

ICONOGRAPHY OF SYNTHESIS

Faced with the stability of these already mixed funerary traditions—'mixed' in the sense that they express in a quasi-classical language (the vine, and the Latin of the accompanying inscriptions) an indigenous religious message—the first manifestations of paleo-Christian art seem to indicate an imported art. These are primarily pieces sculpted in Roman workshops. Sumptuous and heavy, imported at great expense, they were not within the price range of most simple Christians buried under the *tegulae* as in the cemetery of Tarragona. They were commissioned by Lonestiores, like that Leucadius, first minister of the Emperor, whose inscription is surrounded by strigils and by symmetrical scenes showing the bestowal of the keys on Peter and the sacrifice of Abraham. The aristocratic nature of this art is best seen in the mausoleum of Puebla Nueva (Province of Toledo)—an octagonal monument whose dimensions are comparable to those of the tomb of Diocletian at Split. There the crypt contained sumptuous sculpted sarcophagi. One of them, imported from the East (at least as far as its iconography is concerned) during the Theodosian period, presents the acclamation as emperor by the apostles (standing in two symmetrical lines) of Christ enthroned in majesty on a dais, like Theodosius and his sons on the celebrated silver *missorium* of Madrid, found in the last century in Estramadura. The biblical and descriptive iconography of this plastic art of the fourth and fifth centuries is still the privileged expression of a Christian aristocracy with a secular attachment to traditional luxury even in their eternal dwelling-place. Their iconography, in its patterns, is an offshoot of Roman art. There is for example the *acclamatio,* or the unbroken frieze composition of gospel scenes on pieces of the age of Constantine, which has a parallel in the composition and techniques used in the friezes on the Arch of Constantine in Rome. This close symbiosis of the secular iconography of the Empire and Christian religious iconography is typical of the *Christiana tempora* in which Church and Empire gave each other more than mutual support. It is the iconography of a centralized and relatively uniform art, diffused throughout the West (of the towns and rich villas), from the Roman *caput mundi* where it was created.

But already the tetrarchical reorganization had broken the Empire down into vast defensive areas whose internal partition provided the outline of the nations of the future. The 'Spanish Vicariate' established the entire peninsula as a special administrative whole. That reinforced regional and local particularism. Everywhere in the late Empire there was a resurgence of indigenous substrata. With the establishment of Christianity this can be seen in the popularity—especially in Spain—of the cult of the local martyrs about which we have been exceptionally well-informed by the poems in the *Livre des couronnes*. There Prudentius of Calagurris (present-day Calahorra on the upper Ebro) celebrates among others the solider martyrs Emeterius and Chelidonius from his own region, and the local reputation of the healing power of their relics among the Vascones—recently converted and still very close to their *bruta gentilitas* (Prudentius *dixit!*).

Local workshops also appear, like the very curious one at Bureba (a hundred km east of Calahorra). Its modelling technique, schematic and smooth, is comparable to the workmanship on the Hispano-Roman steles of these regions (those of nearby Poza de la Sal, or those of Lara fifty km to the South). The iconography of these local Christian sarcophagi is much more mysterious, and undeciphered if not undecypherable, than that of contemporary Roman imports. There is a *unicum*: the representation of the dream of Perpetua, the third-century Carthaginian martyr who is known to us (dream and all) from the *Passio perpetuae*. There is also a seated figure, carrying a baton, with a bird on his head and another on his baton. As Schlunk has pointed out, this is the legendary election of St Joseph, as recounted in the apocryphal proto-Gospel of St James. In this regard mention has rightly been made of the interest shown in the Apocrypha by the Priscillianist heretics, who were condemned by a council of Saragossa in 380; one of its canons denounced 'separatist' meetings on certain country estates. This group of carvings, in spite of its unique features, brings closer to many indigenous substrata of the northern *meseta*. According to the tenable deductions of Schlunk, the patrons who commissioned them came from a 'Celtic or Ibero-Celtic population, only slightly Romanized at a late date, but probably won over early to Christianity'—no doubt in the course of the third century.

This land of the Autrigones was crossed by the important Roman road that led from Bordeaux to Leon and Astriga by way of Pamplona and Briviesca, but it was hardly urbanized. To the north-west, it is not far to the region of the Cantabri Vadinienses, who in 399 dedicated an altar to the god Erundinus. The trees, birds and rabbits, but also the modes of composition, in the Christian pieces of the Bureba seem to stem directly from the repertoires of ancient funeral iconography in the region. Here we catch a glimpse of the process by which the Christianity of these regions eventually tended towards a synthetic iconography in which the Roman element and its oriental streak coexisted with an *interpretatio christiana* of certain traditional and pre-Christian sacred signs. This was to be confirmed in the seventh century in the small rural churches of the Duera Valley.

RURAL CHURCHES

In the great anarchy of the fifth century, well portrayed in the sombre *Chronicle* of Gallaecus Hydratius de Lamego, Bishop of Chaves (in the north-east of present-day Portugal), superficially-Christianized natives and invading barbarians lived side by side and showed a common hostility to the entrenched Catholic *romanitas* of the towns, while Priscillianism strengthened its positions throughout the north-west. Even though the work of Martin of Braga, at the end of the sixth century, testifies to a struggle against rural paganism and heresy—often in strange combinations—it is nonetheless true that after the political and religious unification of the peninsula by the kings of Toledo, late seventh-century Christian art (as seen, for example, in the churches of Nave, Bande, and Quintanilla) bears witness to a unique integration of Hispanic iconographical traditions.

This integration does no more than superimpose a Christian significance on an entire natural funeral symbolism of transcendence, which was carried over into Visigothic Christianity by those centuries of coexistence to which the Bureba workshop first bears witness in the fourth century. This *interpretatio christiana* simply repeats, in a distinct historical and geographical framework, an operation which, as is agreed today, gave birth to the most ancient Christian iconography (see in this respect the work of T. Klauser and of the Boun school founded by F.-J. Dölger, or of Andre Grabar). Even the *orantes* or the Good Shepherd are not images created *ex nihilo* by the first Christian artists. As much by necessity as by choice, primitive Christian iconography was more often than not crypto-Christian. The problem is not very different in the parallel field of literature. The protreptic nature of the Octavius of Minucius Felix is likewise typically crypto-Christian.

At the heart of the Gothic area of the Province of Zamora, San Pedro de Nava strikingly exemplifies this second stage of cultural absorption in Hispanic Christian iconography. Of its two successive artists, the 'second Master' drew inspiration for the iconography of his capitals and friezes from paleo-Christian sources, probably of eastern derivation: in illuminated bibles, ivories and materials of the Hispanic paleo-Christian tradition, or in Byzantine imports. Its figurative iconography is original but accords with the ultimately Hellenistic and Roman traditions of the most ancient Christian art. Biblical scenes are, e.g., Daniel in the lions' den, the sacrifice of Abraham, various representations of the apostles. Paradisaical ornamentation of Alexandrian provenance: foliated scrolls and grapes with pecking birds, to be reinterpreted within the framework of an evangelical religion, in which the meaning of the parables of the birds of the air and of the vine was familiar to all.

On the other hand, the sculptures of the 'first Master', less skilful and more monotonous, relate to indigenous traditions, both in their formal abstraction and in their symbolic (i.e., non-descriptive) content. Bunches of grapes are schematized into flattened triangles and grouped in cruciform patterns; above all, however, there is a predilection for roses, circles and swastikas. The stripping and restoration of the church has made it possible to recover from its walls an entire series of Asturo-Roman funeral steles bearing the swastika as the only sacred symbol of the heavenly and divine world into which the dead person had passed.

This Christian appropriation of the swastika was all the easier inasmuch as at a very early stage crypto-Christian figurative iconography had interpreted the sun figures as referring to Christ, 'the Sun of justice' announced by the prophet Malachi—whence such a figure as the famous Christ-Apollo on the *arcosolium* near zone P in the cemetery that was uncovered by the excavations at St Peter's in Rome. But here there was no longer any need to allegorize in a crypto-Christian sense the anthropomorphic representations of the sun; for faith in the new 'Sun of justice' found a still more satisfactory vehicle of expression in the ancient swastika, thanks to the transparency of its more abstract symbolism. This sign was destined to survive for a long time in pre-Roman Hispanic art: on the sides of the tenth-century Mozarabic modillions, on the solar stele adopted (and recently rediscovered) in the Cantabrian church built in the same century at Lebena (province of Santander), or on the Mozarabic capitals (so clearly subject to Islamic influence in shape and size) of the main doors of St Millán de la Cogolla (province of Logroño).

This complex meeting of Spanish cultures could and should be studied in many other examples—in the modillions, say, which ratified the dedication of the church of Baños to St John the Baptist by the King of Recesvinthe: the three visible faces of each of these four pieces align the swastika with the conch of the sacred Greco-Roman traditions and a rather primitive carving (as in the representations of animals in the jewels and miniatures of the late Middle Ages) of the dove at the baptism of Christ (in this church dedicated to the baptism there is little doubt about the identification). Or again, in the strange reliefs depicting the Christ-sun and Church-moon (and still bearing the legend SOL and LUNA) in the chapel of Quintanilla de las Viñas—in the heart of the Lara region—the importance and originality of which for the art of the steles I have already stressed. The scheme of the composition (a figure in a cartouche supported by flying angels) copies the ancient tradition in which portraits were supported by two Victories. But the Christian orthodoxy of this celebration in astral metaphors of Christ and the Church is not justified only by a biblical exegesis of the sun and moon, which goes back to the writings of St Ambrose of Milan (fourth century) by way of a chapter in St Isidore of Seville's *Treatise on Nature* (eighth-century Visigothic). *Hic et nunc*, in the Lara region, but in the seventh century (if not at the beginning of the eighth) the choice of such iconography should be regarded in relation not to Manichaeism (the hypothesis has been defended) but, more naturally, to the atavistic attachment of the local Celtic-Iberian peoples to the divine symbolism of the two great lights of heaven, whose symbols their ancestors had, through so many generations, engraved on their tombstones. Finally, we should recall that in the 'dream of Perpetua' on the Bureba sarcophagus mentioned above, heaven is symbolized, in the upper part of the scene, by a double representation of the sun and the moon: a precious new link in the chain of the Christianization of this astral theme.

CHRISTIAN ASSIMILATION OF THE ICONOGRAPHIES

Spain is therefore an especially important field for anyone who wishes to observe the process by which Christianity successively adopted the aesthetic and religious languages of the civilizations in which it had begun to establish itself during the later centuries of antiquity. That privileged position stems from the vast diversity of peoples and cultures which, migrating westwards from Eurasia and Africa by land or sea, came together in what was then the *finis terrae* of the western world. It also stems, in consequence of this, from the extremely heterogeneous stages of development reached by the prehistoric and historic cultures which succeeded, met, confronted and mixed with one another in the Iberian peninsula, from Paleolithic times to the late Middle Ages. There is a prodigious range of sacred art from the caves of Altamira to the Visigothic and Mozarabic churches.

During the period with which we are concerned, this cultural geography appears diverse and complex. In fact one discovers there, along with the remains of a renascent *romanitas*, and coexisting at last in a kingdom unified and reorganized with a nostalgic eye to the Roman archtype, a recrudescence of oriental and more specifically Byzantine influences (partially mediated, as always, by hitherto Roman Africa). But there is also a vitality in the indigenous substrata which profited from the political disasters of the fifth century, from the inadequacy of the Romanization process, and thus, in the north-west, from evangelization—and finally from a certain connivance with the rougher, less advanced civilization of the new immigrant peoples; whether they had passed through the peninsula, like the Vandals, or settled in the country, like the Suevi in Galicia or the Goths in those *campos goticos*, some of the churches of which I have just mentioned: in those Celtic or Celtic-Iberian regions where Romanization had respected, if not encouraged, indigenous cults and epigraphic or plastic expression. The maps drawn up earlier by José María Blázquez, in the first volume of his study of the 'primitive religions of Spain', drew attention immediately to this vitality in the cultures of the 'north-west quarter', within the context of which the present reflections have been made. This Christian assimilation of iconographies followed the course and the vicissitudes first of Romanization and then of evangelization. Progressing from the Roman towns to the more or less Romanized countryside, from being a figurative art it appears to have moved back to being an abstract art, more accessible to more people and better understood through the simplicity of this aesthetic and sacred language, forged through centuries of pre-Christian religion. But one can say equally well that in moving from the concrete to the abstract it has progressed from being an descriptive art, still classical in its anecdotal imitations of nature and history but often 'all-too-human'—even in its representation of biblical *gesta*—to being more mysteriously abstract, and on that account more expressive of an ineffable transcendence. Where our predecessors in the last century saw nothing but a pitiful process of barbarization, we perceive the mysterious passage of a word towards silence. And we, in this century of abstract, if not anti-figurative arts, are far from ill-equipped to understand the profound sense of this evolution, this search for a new language which would be at once more universal, more all-embracing, more accessible to ordinary people, more expressive at a basic level—and as such more open, from the ascetic point of view, to a more purely transcendent revelation, to an Other beyond words, and even beyond images.

Translated by Sarah Fawcett

Bibliography

I. I have given the theme broader treatment, but from a very definite angle, in 'Iconographie et spiritualité dans la culture chrétienne du IVe au VIIe siècle' in *Revue d'histoire de la spiritualité*, Vol. 50 (1974), pp. 285–318 (with a selective bibliography on western Christian iconography by Charles Piétri). For a quick look at the evolution of the Christian arts in the Iberian peninsula during the first ten centuries, see my *Art préroman hispanique* (Geneva, 1973–77): Vol. I: *'Arts paléo-chrétien, wisigothique, asturien'*; Vol. 2: 'Art mozarabe'. For the notion of crypto-Christianity in Latin Christian literature, see my *Aspects et problèmes de la prose d'art au IIIe siècle, La genèse des styles latins chrétiens* (Turin, 1966) (chaptèr iv, on 'Minucius Felix et les valeurs ambigües d'un style crypto-chrétien'). On the historical problems posed by the meeting of the ancient cultures, see the *Acts* of the congress of the Fédération Internationale des Associations d'Etudes Classiques (FIEC), held in Madrid in 1974 on the theme 'Résistance et assimilation aux civilisations classiques', with a good number of contributions on these problems as they relate to ancient Spain (to be published in Bucharest in 1977).

II. Iconography and indigenous Hispano-Roman religions. Start with the works of Antonio García y Bellido (*Esculturas romanas de España y Portugal,* Madrid, 1949) and J. M. Blázquez (*Religiones primitivas de Hispania,* Rome, 1962), and by the same author, *Diccionario de las Religiones preromanas de Hispania* (Madrid, 1975: an expanded edition of his contribution, 'Mythologie dcr alten Hispanier', in H. W. Haussig, *Wörterbuch der Mythologie,* Stuttgart, pp. 207–328), and his articles on the horse and the equestrian hero (in *Ampurias*, Vol. 21, 1939, pp. 281–302, and *Celtiberia*, Vol. 6, 1963, pp. 405–23). The general typology of the steles by A. Lozano Velilla, 'Tipología de las estelas y la población de España', in *Revista de la Universidad Complutense de Madrid*, Vol. 22, no. 86 (1973), pp. 89–114, does not allow one to dispense with such monographs as that of J. C. Elorza, 'Ensayo topográfico de epigrafía romana alavesa' (Victoria, 1967), and 'Estelas romanas en la provincia de Álava' in *Estudios de arquelogía alavesa,* Vol. 4 (1970), pp. 235–74; D. Julia, *Etude épigraphique et iconographique des stèles de Vigo* (Heidelberg, 1971); José A. Abasolo, *Epigrafía romana de la region de Lara de los Infantes* (Burgos, 1974); J. A. Abasolo, M. L. Albertos and J. C. Elorza, *Los monumentas funerarios de época romana, en forma de casa, de la region de Poza de la Sal* (Burgos, 1975). I am grateful to J. M. Blazquez for this reading list.

III. For Paleo-Christian art, start with the works of Pedro de Palol, *Demografía y arqueología hispanicas de los siglos IV al VIII, ensayo de cartografía* (Vallodolid, 1966); *Arqueología cristiana de la España romana (siglos IV–VI)* (Madrid-Vallodolid, 1967); *Arte paleocristiana en España* (Barcelona: very beautiful photographs). On imported sarcophagi: M. Sotomayor, *Sarcófagos romano-cristianos de España, Estudio iconográfico* (Granada, Facultad de Teología, 1975) (a second volume on the local workshops has been announced). On the la Bureba workshop: Helmut Schlunk, 'Zu den früchristliches Sarkophagen aus der Bureba (prov. Burgos)' in *Madrider Mitteilungen*, Vol. 6 (1965), pp. 139–66; and 'Die frühchristlichen Denkmaler aus der Nordwestern der iberischen Halbinsel', in *Legio VII Gemina* (Leon, 1970), pp. 475–509. On the paleo-Christian culture of north-western Spain at the beginning of the fifth century, see my 'Le distique du chrismon de Quiroga: sources littéraires et contexte spirituel', in *Archivo Español de Arqueología,* Vols. 45–47 (1974), pp. 557–85.

IV. On Visigothic decoration, its sources and its religious significance, there is useful material in J. Puig y Cadafalch, *L'art wisigothique et ses survivances. Recherches sur les origines et le développement de l'art en France et en Espagne du IVe au XIIIe siècle* (Paris, 1961) (the manuscript was ready in 1944). The best work of synthesis on Visigothic art is still that of Helmut Schlunk: 'Arte visigodo', in *Ars Hispaniae* (Madrid, 1947), pp. 227–323, after the earlier one contributed by E. Camps Cazorla and J. Ferrandis to the *Historia de España* edited by R. Menéndez Pidal (Madrid, 1940), pp. 433–666. See also P. de Palol, *Arte hispanico de época visigoda* (Barcelona, 1968). For the primacy of the ancient traditions in this art, see P. de Palol, 'Esencia del arte hispanico de época visigoda: romanismo y germanismo', in the *Settimane* of Spoleto, Vol. 3 (1956). For the literary aspects of the meeting of cultures in Spain at the beginning of the seventh century, see part 6, chapter 5, 'La culture isidorienne dans l'Occident contemporain', of my *Isidore de Seville et la culture classique dans L'Espagne visigothique*, Vol. 2 (Paris, 1959), pp. 831–62.

Irénée-Henri Dalmais

The Celebration of
the Christmas Cycle
in the Eastern Churches

PRE-CHRISTIAN ROOTS OF CHRISTIAN FEASTS

THERE is a long tradition in most Christian communities that has led them to regard the liturgy as a virtually intangible complex of celebrations whose recurrence structures the various cycles of existence. The annual feasts mark the passing of the seasons, to the point where we now scarcely distinguish between those that commemorate an historical event, or, like Easter, plumb the mysteries of the history of salvation, and those whose establishment owes more to the rhythms of nature herself, particularly as observed in predominantly agricultural communities. Liturgy—the name itself should remind us— reaches the heart of a community's will to live together, what makes it tell itself what essentially it means by calling itself a community, what makes it reach out through time and space to embrace all those it considers like-minded.

This is why we should feel no surprise at the sense of unease and shock, even rupture, produced by any change in rites or calendar. There are numerous precedents for the situation in Catholic communities produced by the changes to the Roman rite introduced by Vatican II. In the Orthodox tradition, there was the *raskol* schism with its tragic consequences, brought about by the liturgical reforms of Patriarch Nikon in seventeenth-century Russia; more recently, the schism in Greece produced by the introduction of the 'new calendar', resisted for fifty years by the adherents of the 'Julian calendar'. The other reason for the deep disturbances caused is the difficulty of distinguishing what is of properly Christian significance in a feast from what its mode of celebration has acquired over the years from the human context in which it is set. The best-known, as well as the most complex and richest example of this is of course Easter. Between the second and the fourth centuries, it would seem to have been the only Christian feast: according to Tertullian, its celebration lasted fifty days, till Pentecost. The rites associated with its Jewish origin were soon neglected: not only the eating of the whole lamb, which was only sacrificed in Jerusalem, but all the customs belonging to the seder meal, including the basic rule—that only unleavened bread should be eaten. On the other hand, Christians from very early times celebrated Easter in a short *triduum*, starting on the Thursday evening and ending at dawn on the Sunday. This brought in a rhythm of passing from darkness to light, particularly rich in symbolism at the spring equinox and the full phase of the moon. This symbolism of light, related to the manifest glory of the risen Christ, later found expression in a variety of rites, such as the solemnization of the Lucernary in the liturgy of the Paschal candle in the West, and the entry into the church by candlelight during the Easter vigil in the East. And, little by little, extra-liturgical usages were added, generally prolonging very ancient customs related to the unfolding of the solar cycle.

These elements are still, however, secondary and fairly extrinsic to the Paschal celebration properly so called, which is perhaps why this sometimes seems less of a popular feast, at least to western Christians, who have difficulty in assimilating it to the rhythms of their existence. This is why I have chosen to centre these observations rather on the ensemble of celebrations organized round the theme of the Nativity-Manifestation (Epiphany) of Christ as observed by 'eastern' Christians, in particular the Coptic Church of Egypt, which very early on gave them a form rooted in an immemorial past, but still living and developed more and more richly as time went on.

THE ORIGINS OF THE FEASTS OF THE NATIVITY AND THE EPIPHANY

The obscurity surrounding the origins and original meaning of these feasts is well known. It is only towards the middle of the fourth century that we find the first well-attested evidence for their celebration. By then, in Rome—and apparently for most of Latin Christendom—the date had been fixed at December 25. On that date, according to the evidence of the *Cronograph* of 354, a feast of the unconquered sun (*Sol invictus*) was celebrated, at least since the dedication of the temple built on the Field of Mars in 274 by order of the Emperor Aurelian. In the middle of the fifth century, St Leo still found it necessary to protest against the gestures of superstitious veneration that Christians addressed to the rising sun before entering the Basilica of St Peter. According to a Paschal computation, a system had been worked out, by which the creation of the world—or at least the creation of light—was dated on March 25, the same date therefore as the conception of Christ, an additional reason for placing his birth date at December 25. Mgr Duchesne gives considerable importance to these speculations, perhaps too much so, as Dom Bernard Botte considers.[1] However this may be, a cycle centred on the winter solstice was a great spur to popularization of the feast of Christmas in the western Church, in the Nordic countries in particular, with their proliferation of customs associated with celebration of the lengthening days. In the East, however, its influence was hardly felt, even though most of them—with the exception of the Armenian Church—fairly quickly accepted the date of December 25 as that of the Nativity of Christ, and integrated it with their own cycle of celebration of the Manifestation of the Lord, for which the date of January 6 had already been established.

The choice of this date is even more difficult to explain than that of December 25. And yet its implications have proved to be so varied and so rich that they assured this feast a wealth of doctrinal and spiritual content that it has never known in the West, a wealth that could not but enrich the celebrations of December 25, which soon became accepted as historical fact. Consequently, while in the West the feast of Christmas was soon surrounded with more or less folkloric customs with but extrinsic significance—which enabled it to become de-Christianized—the very different development of the feast of the Epiphany in the East, carrying the Nativity with it, so to speak, continued along very definitely Christian lines, even while dipping deep into the pre-Christian past of various civilizations.

THE CELEBRATION OF THE MANIFESTATION OF THE LORD IN THE COPTIC CHURCH AND ITS PRE-CHRISTIAN ANTECEDENTS

Egypt played a dominant role in the course of these developments, and perhaps at their outset too. Even today, it is undoubtedly in the Coptic Church of Egypt—and in that of Ethiopia, which owes so much to Egypt while developing traditions received from elsewhere in its own manner—that the vast cycle of celebrations surrounding the Nativity and the Epiphany has remained most popular.

Greco-Roman Egypt, crossroads of civilizations and home of syncretism, while still firmly attached—one must not forget—to the perpetuation of its own unchanging rites and the transmission of its own ancient traditions, was intensely responsive to evocation of the great cosmic archetypes. They re-appear constantly in early allusions to Christian celebrations of the Nativity and Manifestation of the Lord Christ, 'Emmanuel, our God, our King', as the Coptic tradition likes to acclaim him. On this point, the publication of the great inscription giving the rites observed in the temple of Denderah for the celebration of the 'Mysteries of Osiris' in the first centuries of our era, with the commentary by Emile Chasseriat, is particularly informative.[2]

In his effort to establish a chronology of Christ on the basis of the dates given in Luke in relation to his baptism, Clement of Alexandria mentions that: 'the followers of Basilides also celebrate the baptism of Jesus, and spend the whole of the night before in reading the Scriptures. According to them, this took place in the fifteenth year of the reign of Tiberius, on the fifteenth—or, others say, the eleventh—day of the month of Tubi (the tenth or the sixth of January)' (Str. I. 21; 146. 1–2). But he gives no reason for the choice of this date in certain Gnostic circles. More descriptive, a century and a half later, Epiphanius of Salamis gives this justification of his chronology: 'The Saviour was born in the forty-second year of Augustus king of the Romans, during the consulate of the same Octavius Augustus for the thirteenth time, and that of Sylvan, as attested by the consular records of the Romans. This is what is found: during the consulate of these two, that is Octavius for the thirteenth time and Sylvan, the Christ was born on the eighth day of the Ides of January, thirteen days after the winter solstice and the beginning of the growth of light. This date is feted by the Hellenes, that is, by idolaters, on the eighth day of the Kalends of January, called Saturnalia by the Romans, Kronia by the Egyptians and Kikellia by the Alexandrians. This is the day on which the change occurs, that is the solstice, from when the day begins to lengthen, with light receiving an increase; it then accomplishes the number of thirteen days till the eighth day of the Ides of January, till the date of the birth of Christ, the thirtieth part of an hour being added each day'.

These somewhat convoluted explanations are evidently aimed at explaining how the feast of January 6 can be reconciled to the solstice and to the celebration—just becoming general—of the birth of Christ on the day of the 'Sol invictus'. But in fact the perspective was somewhat different in the circles in which Epiphanius moved, as these references a little later show: 'There have been, and still are, many other facts to serve as witness and support of this fact, by which I refer to the birth of Christ. For the chiefs of the worship of idols are forced to recognize a part of the truth and, being liars, in order to deceive the idolaters who place their trust in them, make in many places a great feast on this same night of the Epiphany, so that those who believe in error will not seek out the truth. First of all, in Alexandria, in what is called the Koreion—which is a very great temple, the sanctuary of Kore —they keep vigil all night, venerating their idol with songs and the sound of flutes. When their vigil ends at cockcrow, they go down with torches into an underground place and bring from it a wooden statue of a naked seated figure, bearing a gilt mark in the shape of a cross on its forehead, two other similar marks on its hands, and two more on its knees, all five being gilt in the same manner. They carry the statue round the temple seven times to the sound of flutes, tambourines and hymns, and having venerated it in this way, they take it back to the underground place. And when asked what this mystery means, they reply: Today, at this hour, Kore, that is the Virgin, has given birth to the *Aeon*. This also takes place in Petra—the metropolis of Arabia that is the Eden of the Scriptures—where they sing to the Virgin in the Arabic tongue, calling her Chamaan, which means girl or virgin, and her son Douzares, which means only son of the Lord. It also happens in Elousa the same night as in Alexandria and Petra'.

A little further on, he recounts other prodigies, some attested elsewhere, supposed to belong to the same date, and which he relates to the miracle at Cana: 'According to the Egyptians, the birth of the Lord according to the flesh took place on the eleventh day of Tubi, and on the same day, thirty years later, the miracle at Cana in Galilee, changing water into wine, was performed. This is why the divine prodigy that took place then is reproduced in many places in our time, as the unbelievers witness; so in many places they witness springs and rivers changed into wine. It is so with the spring of Cybira, a town in Caria, at the time when the servers draw and one says: Give the wine to the master of the feast. The fountain at Gerasa gives the same testimony. We have drunk from the spring at Cybira and our brothers from the fountain at Gerasa in the Martyrium. And in Egypt many claim the same for the Nile. Also on the eleventh of Tubi according to the Egyptians, all go to draw water and put it on one side in Egypt and in many other countries (*Panarion*, 51. 22–30. *Ed*. GCS. 31, pp. 284–301, *trad*. B. Botte, *op. cit.*, pp. 68–72).

Whatever the origin and value of the information complacently collected by the credulous Epiphanius, it does at least bear witness to the ancient origin of customs that persist down to our own time in the various Churches of the East, and particularly in Egypt. While Cassian is the first to attest specifically, around the year 400, to a feast celebrated in Egypt on January 6 commemorating both the Nativity of Christ and his Baptism (*Coll*. X. 2; PL49, 820–21; *CSEL*, 13, 286–87), it seems certain enough that the usage dates further back, and that the concept is a wider one embracing the Manifestation of the Lord, evoked by a variety of usages rooted in a past still particularly evocative for a people exceptionally attached to conservation of the customs of the Ancients while giving them a new meaning.

On this aspect, Georges Coquin, in his monograph, *Les origines de l'Epiphanie en Egypte*,[3] contributes new elements whilst opening a number of highly interesting perspectives unnoticed by Botte. First there is a text from the *Canons of Athanasius*, which he claims to be able to date from the early decades of the fourth century: after a recommendation to his bishop that no Sunday or feast-day of the Lord should pass without gathering together the needy for a distribution of alms, this text continues: 'The bishop should also rejoice with them on the feast of the Manifestation of the Lord, which is in the month of Tuba, that is, the Baptism. . . . The Egyptians call this the feast of the beginning of the Year. The Hebrews called Easter Day the beginning of the year, that is the first of the month of Barmûda (March 27). It is also in the month of Tuba that our Saviour showed himself to be God, by changing water into wine in an astonishing miracle'.[4] Referring to works on the cult of the Nile,[5] Coquin sees in this the origin of particular customs, particularly those mentioned by Epiphanius, which would have spread from Egypt throughout eastern Christendom and even reached some parts of the West. He can produce documents that mention such festivities taking place in the month of Tubi, related to developments in the cult of Osiris, celebrated throughout the preceding month of Kohiak, developments that were soon to leave their mark on the Christian calendar. Egyptian conservatism, coupled with the vagaries of their calendar, kept celebrations originally related to the rising of the Nile (July-August) on dates that had gone out of fashion. These celebrations consisted of a vigil with torches, which led to them being referred to as the 'Feast of lights', a name often given in the East to the Epiphany and which cannot otherwise be explained. At dawn, there was a procession to the river bank, where the 'hole of the spring' (Greek *phiale*) had been dug, from which the life-giving water could be drawn. The statue of the Nile and a pot for the sacred water were borne in procession, and the people carried palm branches and reeds. Then, having drunk the regenerating water and given thanks for this gift of life in the temple, they gave themselves up to celebrations all along the river bank. We also know that the hieroglyph for 'life', the *ankh*, the Osirian sign *par excellence*, was not unlike a cross, which explains the marks of the cross mentioned by Epiphanius.

ARABIC SOURCES OF THE FATIMID ERA

It is a remarkable fact that descriptions of the Coptic rites of Christmas and the Epiphany found in Arabic writers of the Fatimid era (ninth to thirteenth centuries) give a very similar account. They were collected by Al-Maqrizi during the first half of the fifteenth century, at a particularly dark time for the Copts. Here is his description of the Nativity, on the 29th of Kohiak, which originally corresponded to December 25: 'They (the Copts) keep vigil from the evening of the night before the Nativity and have the custom of lighting a very large number of lights in their churches and decorating them. In Egypt this feast is celebrated on the 29th day of the month of Kohiak. Till now, it has remained one of the most solemn feasts of the year. Under the Fatimites, Cairo pastries, cakes made from flour, others of julep, dishes of fritters, and of the fish known as mullet, were served to high dignitaries, great stewards, emirs with collar of office, secretaries and others. The fire game is a custom of the Christians on the day of the Nativity. . . . We have witnessed Christmas in Cairo, Misr, and throughout Egypt become an occasion of magnificent solemnity. Candles decorated with pretty colours and delightful images were sold for considerable sums. No one, however high or low his station, failed to buy some for his children and family. These lights were called *faounis, fanous* in the singular. The stalls in the bazaars were hung with great quantities of them, of considerable beauty. There was a veritable fever to bump their prices up, to the extent that I have seen one originally priced at a thousand or perhaps five hundred silver *dirhems* rise to more than seventy gold *mithqâl*. Even the beggars in the streets took part in these festivities: they prayed to God to be given a *fanous*, and people bought them little tapers worth a *dirhem* or so. Later, the Egyptian troubles that caused so many luxurious customs to disappear, ruined the Christmas *fanous* trade, of which little trace remains'.[6]

Such customs, however, have a way of surviving vicissitudes. At the present time the Christmas lights flourish again in all their former glory, beyond the confines of Egypt, which seems to have been their most durable home, as well as perhaps their original one. Christmas in the East, as well as in the West, and to an even greater extent, is a festival of light, or rather of flame. In this respect, there is a particularly interesting custom of the Syrian (Jacobite) Church, newly re-established in India, starting in Kerala, observed at the same time of the year. The long Christmas vigil, held to the sound of hymns to St Ephraim and St James of Saroug, comes to an end towards dawn with a procession to a bonfire of aromatic branches, which is then solemnly lit, and on which all those present scatter grains of incense, while the clergy recite prayers, in homage to Him who is the Light of the world. This is a particularly evocative symbol in eastern countries.

The Epiphany, however, is the true 'Festival of Lights', the name given to it by St Gregory Nazianzen as far back as the fourth century. Various explanations for the name have been proposed, none entirely convincing. It would seem that once again we have to look to Egypt, as the pre-Christian customs evoked by Epiphanius would suggest. The description of the Coptic celebration of the Epiphany given by Al-Maqrizi, ten centuries later, show how faithfully these customs had been preserved. He calls it the feast of the Immersion or Baptism (*Denh*): 'This feast is celebrated in Egypt on the eleventh day of the month of Tuba. The origin of the feast is that Yahia ben Zakaria (John son of Zachary), blessed be he, whom the Christians call John the Baptist, baptised the Christ, that is washed him in the lake of Jordan. And when the Christ, blessed be he, emerged from the water, the Holy Spirit came down upon him. This is why the Christians immerse their children and themselves in water on that date. This ceremony always takes place at the coldest time of the year. It is called the feast of the Immersion, and was formerly celebrated with the greatest solemnity. Al-Massoudi (in 942) describes it in these terms in his *Fields of Gold*[7]: The night of the Immersion was a very great feast for the inhabitants of Misr (old Cairo). No one went to bed that night. It was the night of the eleventh day of Tuba. Mohammad ibn-Toghj l'Ikchid was in his palace in Misr, built on an island surrounded by the Nile. He caused a thousand torches to be lit on the edge of the isle and the Festât bank, besides the lamps and torches lit by the people of Misr. There were thousands of people there on the banks of the Nile that night, Moslems and Christians, the former in boats, the latter in houses along both banks of the Nile. Nothing that could make a show was omitted: food, drink, clothes, gold and silver musical instruments, jewels and trinkets, music and good cheer. It was the greatest night Misr had ever seen, the night of most pleasure. The roads were not closed that night. Most of those present immersed themselves in the Nile; they claim this is a safeguard against bodily ailments as well as a talisman against sickness'.

Al-Maqrizi continues with another description, a little later, but still belonging to the splendiferous Fatimid epoch: 'Al-Masihi tells in his account of the year 367 [A.D. 978] that the Christians were forbidden to observe the usual customs associated with the Immersion—grouping together, going down into the water and amusing themselves; the warning was given that anyone disobeying this injunction would be punished with immediate banishment. The same author relates that the feast of Immersion was celebrated in the year 388 [A.D. 999]. Tents and pavilions were set up and seats placed at several points along the bank of the Nile. Divans were placed for the Raïs ibn-Ibrahim the Christian, secretary of the Barjaouân *oustâdh*, lamps and torches were lit in his honour, and there was singing and miming. He set to drinking till the time for his immersion, then bathed and retired'. A little further on, we find: 'The same author recounts the following for the year 415 [A.D. 1026]: the immersion of the Christians took place on the night of Wednesday, the fourth day of Dhou'l-Qa'da. The custom of selling fruit, mutton and other provisions had spread. The Prince of the Believers Az-Zahir li-l'Zaz-Din-illah came down to the castle of his grandfather Al'-Aziz bi'llah in Misr to see the immersion, bringing his harem with him. The Moslems were forbidden to mix with the Christians when they went down into the waters of the Nile. Badrad-Daoula, the black slave in charge of the two police forces, set up his tent near the bridge and took his place in it. The Prince of Believers lit lamps and torches throughout the night and there was a brilliant show of light. Then monks and priests came with candles and crosses, carrying out a long service till the hour for Immersion came'.[8]

SOME POPULAR CUSTOMS OF OTHER EASTERN CHURCHES

This wealth of quotations, plus the evident interest the author takes in them, shows how popular these ceremonies still were even after Egypt had become predominantly Moslem, and how their Christian character was not disputed, even though they contained a number of elements dating from a pre-Christian past. As we know, these popular rites of 'immersion' spread through the various Christian civilizations of the East, particularly, despite the rigours of the climate, to the Slav countries. In the Orthodox countries, while as many people as possible went to celebrate the sanctification of the waters beside a river or lake, or on the seashore, the Christian content of the ceremonies was augmented by the custom of throwing a precious cross into the waters—which the best swimmers then hastened to recover.

Ethiopia, which culturally owes so much to Coptic Egypt, shows the feast of the Baptism (*Tamkat*) at its most spectacular. There customs held in common with other Churches are enriched with the sacred dances of the *Dabtaras* (singer-scribes), and the special rite of each year baptising the *tabet* (boards) which in each church represent the Ark of the Covenant, carried, in popular tradition, to Axum. So it is there that the ceremony, enacted in the sacred pool of the 'Baths of the Queen of Sheba', displays the most pomp. This is perhaps the clearest example of the interaction of properly Christian ceremony with a host of popular usages stemming from a variety of sources.

The offices proper to the month of Kohiak, so dear to Coptic piety, on the other hand, are purely Christian in character. This month, ending with Christmas, had from long past been consecrated to Osiris, and, in Syncretic Greco-Roman Egypt, his cult and that of Isis were frequently fused with those of Hator and Orus. This was particularly true of the shrines of Edfou and Denderah, where the rites of the mysteries of Osiris were developed. There is certainly no continuity between them and the Coptic celebrations, developed relatively late, in which praises of the Virgin Mother of God are sung throughout the month of Kohiak. But it is equally true that these draw inspiration from the tradition of a whole race, of celebrating the rebirth of light and of the water that gives life at this time of the year.

Translated by Paul Burns

Notes

1. B. Botte, 'Les origines de la Noël et de l'Epiphanie: étude historique', in Coll. *Textes et Études liturgiques* (Louvain, 1932), p. 60.

2. E. Chassériat, 'Le mystère d'Osiris au mois de Kohiak', in *Coll. Institut français d'archéologie orientale*, 2 fasc. (Cairo, 1966–68).

3. R. G. Coquin, 'Les origines de l'Epiphanie en Egypte', in *Lex Orandi* 40 (Paris, 1967), pp. 139–70.

4. *Op. cit.*, p. 155. Text edited by Riedel-Crum (London, 1904), pp. 20–1.

5. *Ibid.*, p. 163, referring to D. Bonneau, *La crue du Nil, divinité égyptienne, à travers mille ans d'histoire: 332 B.C.-641 A.D.* (Paris, 1964).

6. Tiqi Ed-din Al-Maqrizi, 'The Coptic feasts', in *PO* X, 4, pp. 321–22.

7. *Les prairies d'or*, Fr. tr. (Paris, 1863), II, p. 364.

8. *PO*, X, 4, pp. 322–25.

Virgil Elizondo

Our Lady of Guadalupe as a Cultural Symbol: 'The Power of the Powerless'

NOWADAYS we realize that religious symbols which the theologian
has labled as 'popular' religion and has looked upon as a species of
pagan practice do not have to be rejected, but reinterpreted. In past
decades the tendency of rational theology was to consider symbols as
fantasies; to underline their ambiguity; and therefore to speak of them
only in negative terms. This leads to an opposition between the religion
of the people, which is not looked upon as true faith, and faith in
Christ, which appears as the religion of the intellectual elite. A closer
view of reality leads to a different understanding.[1] Even to the theologian, popular devotion appears ambiguous; nevertheless, it is the way
the people relate to the God of Jesus. Therefore, from the pastoral as
well as from the theological point of view, we have to try to answer the
following question: What is the meaning of popular symbols and how
do they function in relation to the Gospel? In this article I try to clarify
the problem by considering one of the most important living symbols
of the Catholicism of the Americas: our Lady of Guadalupe.

If our Lady of Guadalupe had not appeared, the collective struggles
of the Mexican people to find meaning in their chaotic existence would
have created her. The cultural clash[2] of sixteenth-century Spain and
Mexico was reconciled in the brown Lady of Tepeyac[3] in a way no
other symbol can rival. In her the new Mestizo[4] race, born of the
violent encounter between Europe and indigenous America, finds its
meaning, uniqueness, and unity. Guadalupe is the key to understanding

25

the Christianity of the New World[5] and the Christian consciousness of the Mexicans and the Mexican Americans of the United States.

HISTORICAL CONTEXT OF THE APPARITION

To appreciate the profound meaning of Guadalupe it is important to know the historical setting at the time of the apparition. Suddenly an exterior force, the white men of Europe, intruded on the closely-knit and well-developed system of time-space relationships of the pre-Columbian civilizations.[6] Neither had ever heard of the other, nor had any suspicion that the other group existed. Western historiographers have studied the conquest from the justifying viewpoint of the European colonizers, but there is another aspect, that of the conquered. With the conquest, the world of the indigenous peoples of Mexico had, in effect, come to an end. The final battles in 1521 were not just a victory in warfare, but the end of a civilization. At first, some tribes welcomed the Spaniards and joined them in the hope of being liberated from Aztec domination. Only after the conquest did they discover that the defeat of the Aztecs was in effect the defeat of all the natives of their land.[7] This painful calvary of the Mexican people began when Cortez landed on Good Friday, April 22, 1519; it ended with the final battle on August 13, 1521. It was a military as well as a theological overthrow, for their capital had been conquered, their women violated, their temples destroyed, and their gods defeated.

We cannot allow the cruelty of the conquest to keep us from appreciating the heroic efforts of the early missioners. Their writings indicated that it was their intention to found a new Christianity more in conformity with the Gospel, not simply a continuation of that in Europe. They had been carefully prepared by the universities of Spain. Immediate efforts were made to evangelize the native Mexicans. The life style of the missioners, austere poverty and simplicity, was in stark contrast to that of the conquistadors. Attempts were made to become one with the people and to preach the Gospel in their own language and through their customs and traditions. Yet the missioners were limited by the socio-religious circumstances of their time. Dialogue was severely limited, for neither side understood the other. The Spaniards judged the Mexican world from within the categories of their own Spanish world vision. Iberian communication was based on philosophical and theological abstractions and direct, precise speech. The missioners were convinced that truth in itself was sufficient to bring rational persons to conversion. They were not aware of the totally different way of communicating truth, especially divine truth, which could only be adequately communicated through flower and song.[8]

Even the best of the missioners could not penetrate the living temple of the Mexican consciousness. This was also the time of the first *audiencia* of Guzmán which was noted for its corruption and abuses of the Indians. During this period the Church was in constant conflict with the civil authorities because of their excessive avarice, corruption, and cruel treatment of the natives. The friars were good men who gradually won the love and respect of the common people. However, the religious convictions of generations would not give way easily, especially those of a people who firmly believed that the traditions of their forefathers were the way of the gods. However, as the friars tried to convert the wise men of the Indians by well-prepared theological exposition, the Indians discovered that the friars were in effect trying to eliminate the religion of their ancestors. The shock of human sacrifices led many of the missioners to see everything else in the native religion as diabolical, while the shock of the Spaniards' disregard for life by killing in war kept the Indians from seeing anything good or authentic in the conquerors' religion. The Indians would take captives to be sacrificed, but they would never kill directly in war. The mutual scandal made communication difficult.[9] Furthermore, the painful memory of the conquest and new hardships imposed upon the Indians made listening to a 'religion of love' difficult. Efforts to communicate remained at the level of words, but never seemed to penetrate to the level of the symbols of the people, which contained the inner meanings of their world vision. For the Indians these attempts at conversion by total rupture with the ways of their ancestors were a deeper form of violence than the physical conquest itself. Christianity had in some fashion been brought over, but it had not yet been implanted. The Indians and missioners heard each other's words but interpretation was at a standstill. Many heroic efforts were made, but little fruit had been produced. The missioners continued in prayer and self-sacrifice to ask for the ability to communicate the Gospel.

THE APPARITION AND ITS MEANING

In 1531, ten years after the conquest, an event happened whose origins are clouded in mystery, yet its effects have been monumental and continuous. Early documentation about what happened does not exist, yet the massive effect which the appearance of our Lady of Guadalupe had and continues to have on the Mexican people cannot be denied. The meaning of the happening has been recorded throughout the years in the collective memory of the people. Whatever happened in 1531 is not past history but continues to live, to grow in meaning, and to influence the lives of millions today.

According to the legend, as Juan Diego, a Christianized Indian of common status, was going from his home in the *barriada* near Tepeyac, he heard beautiful music. As he approached the source of the music, a lady appeared to him and speaking in Nahuatl, the language of the conquered, she commanded Juan Diego to go to the palace of the archbishop of Mexico at Tlatelolco and to tell him that the Virgin Mary, 'Mother of the true God through whom one lives' wanted a temple to be built at that site so that in it she 'can show and give forth all my love, compassion, help, and defence to all the inhabitants of this land . . . to hear their lamentations and remedy their miseries, pain, and sufferings'. After two unsuccessful attempts to convince the bishop of the Lady's authenticity, the Virgin wrought a miracle. She sent Juan Diego to pick roses in a place where only desert plants existed. She arranged the roses in his cloak and sent him to the archbishop with the sign he had demanded. As Juan Diego unfolded his cloak in the presence of the archbishop, the roses fell to the ground and the image of the Virgin appeared on his cloak. The Mexican people came to life again because of Guadalupe. The response of the Indians was a spontaneous explosion of pilgrimages, festivals, and conversions to the religion of the Virgin. Out of their meaningless and chaotic existence of the post-conquest years, a new meaning erupted. The immediate response of the Church ranged from silence to condemnation. Early sources indicated that the missioners, at least those who were writing, were convinced that it was an invention of the Indians and an attempt to re-establish their previous religion. Yet gradually the Church accepted the apparition of Guadalupe as the Virgin Mary, Mother of God. In 1754 Pope Benedict XIV officially recognized the Guadalupe tradition by bringing it into the official liturgy of the Church.[10]

To understand the response of Juan Diego and the Mexican people it is necessary to view the event not through western categories of thought but through the system of communication of the Nahuatls of that time. What for the Spanish was an apparition for the conquered and dying Mexican nation was the re-birth of a new civilization. The details of the image conveyed a profound meaning to the Indian peoples. Upon reading the legend, the first striking detail is that Juan Diego heard beautiful music, which alone was enough to establish the heavenly origin of the Lady. For the Indians, music was the medium of divine communication. The Lady appeared on the sacred hill of Tepeyac, one of the four principal sacrificial sites in Meso america. It was the sanctuary of Tonantzin, the Indian virgin mother of the gods. The dress was a pale red, the colour of the spilled blood of sacrifices and the colour of Huitzilopopchtli, the god who gave and preserved life. The blood of the Indians had been spilled on Mexican soil and fertilized mother earth, and now something new came forth. Red was also the colour for the East, the direction from which the sun arose victorious after it had died for the night. The predominant colour of the portrait is the blue-green of the mantle, which was the royal colour of the Indian gods. It was also the colour of Ometéotl, the origin of all natural forces. In the colour psychology of the native world, blue-green stood at the centre of the cross of opposing forces and signified the force unifying the opposing tensions at work in the world. One of the prophetic omens which the native wise men interpreted as a sign of the end of their civilization was the appearance, ten years before the conquest, of a large body of stars in the sky. The stars had been one of the signs of the end, and now the stars in her mantle announced the beginning of a new era. Being supported by heavenly creatures could have meant two, not necessarily contradictory, things. First, that she came on her own and, therefore, was not brought over by the Spaniards. Second, the Indians saw each period of time as supported by a god. This was recorded by a symbol representing the era being carried by a lesser creature. The Lady carried by heavenly creatures marked the appearance of a new era. The Lady wore the black band of maternity around her waist, the sign that she was with child. She was offering her child to the New World. The Lady was greater than the greatest in the native pantheon because she hid the sun but did not extinguish it. The sun god was their principal deity, and she was more powerful. The Lady was also greater than their moon god, for she stood upon the moon, yet did not crush it. However, great as this Lady was, she was not a goddess. She wore no mask as the Indian gods did, and her vibrant, compassionate face in itself told anyone who looked upon it that she was the compassionate mother.

Now the fullness of the apparition developed with the Lady's request for a temple. In the Indian hieroglyphic recordings of the conquest, a burning, destroyed temple was the sign of the end of their civilization and way of life. Therefore, the request for the temple was not just for a building where her image could be venerated, but for a new way of life. It would express continuity with their past and yet radically transcend that past. One civilization had indeed ended, but now another one was erupting out of their own mother soil.

Not only did the Lady leave a powerful message in the image, but the credentials she chose to present herself to the New World were equally startling. For the bishop, the roses from the desert were a startling phenomenon; for the Indians, they were the sign of new life. Flowers and music to them were the supreme way of communication through which the presence of the invisible, all-powerful God could be expressed. As the apparition had begun with music, giving it an atmosphere of the divine, it reached its peak with flowers, the sign of life beyond life, the sign that beyond human suffering and death there was something greater-than-life in the dwelling place of the giver of life.[11]

The narration as it exists today does not appear to be historical, at least in the western scientific understanding of the word. It is not based on objective, verifiable, written documentation. However, it is a historical narrative to the people who have recorded their past through this specific literary genre.[12] Furthermore, popular religion has often been too easily labelled by outsiders, especially sociologists and theologians of the dominant groups, as alienating and superstitious of its very nature. Popular piety is not necessarily and of itself alienating; in fact, for a defeated, conquered and colonized people, it serves as a final resistance against the way of the powerful. Popular religiosity becomes alienating when agents of religion use it to legitimize and maintain the *status quo*. However, it becomes liberating when used as a source of unity and strength in the struggle for dignity and subsequent change against the powerful of society. It is the collective voice of the dominated people crying out: 'We will not be eliminated; we will live on! We have been conquered, but we will not be destroyed'. In the first stages, it gives meaning to an otherwise meaningless existence and thus a reason for living. As the triumphant group has its way of recording history, so those who have been silenced by subjugation have their interpretation of the past. Their accounts exist in an even deeper way. For the defeated and powerless, history is recorded and lived in the collective memory of the people: their songs, dances, poetry, art, legends, and popular religion. For the powerful, history is only a written record, while for the defeated, history is life, for it is the memory that keeps telling them that things are not as they ought to be. This memory cannot be destroyed or opposed by the powerful because they do not understand it. Accordingly it is not surprising that in the history of Mexico there is no place for the Tepeyac tradition. Guadalupe, the most persistent influence in Mexico, is found only in the folklore and popular religious practices of the masses.

At the time of the apparition, the Spanish were building churches over the ruins of the Aztec temples. The past grandeur and power of Tenochtitlán-Tlatelolco (the original name of present-day Mexico City) was being transformed into the glory of new Spain. Juan Diego dared to go to the centre of power and with supranatural authority (as the Lady commanded) demanded that the powerful should change their plans and build a temple—a symbol of a new way of life—not within the grandeur of the city, in accordance with the plans of Spain, but within the *barriada* of Tepeyac in accordance with the desires of the people. The hero of the story is a simple conquered Indian from the *barriada* who is a symbol of the poor and oppressed refusing to be destroyed by the dominant group. The purpose of the story was to convert the archbishop, the symbol of the new Spanish power group, and to turn the attention of the conquering group from building up the rich and powerful centre, governments, knowledge and religion, to the periphery of society where the people continued to live in poverty and misery.

The narration is only a wrapping for the continuing struggle of the masses for survival and liberation from the imposition of the ways of the powerful which has been going on for the past 400 years. Through unceasing struggle, a dynamic tradition has emerged from the primitive story. This tradition has come to stand for the dignity, identity, unity, personal and collective emancipation, and the liberation movements of the Mexican people. Miguel Hidalgo fought for Mexican independence under the banner of our Lady of Guadalupe. Emiliano Zapata led his agrarian reform under her protection, and today Cesar Chavez battles against one of the most powerful economic blocks in the United States under the banner of our Lady of Guadalupe; and he is succeeding in his struggle for justice against all human odds. This tradition was relegated to the area of fable or legend not because it was lacking in historical veracity, but precisely because its living historical veracity cannot be fully accepted by the powerful political, economic, educational, sociological, or religious élite of any moment of history. The full truth of Tepeyac is the obvious disturbing truth of the millions of poor, powerless, peripheral oppressed of our society. The significance of Guadalupe is the voice of the masses calling upon the élite to leave their economic, social, political and religious thrones of pseudo-security and work with them—within the *movimientos de la base*—in transforming society into a more human place for everyone. It was through the presence of our Lady of Guadalupe that the possibility of cultural dialogue began. The missioners' activity had won a basis of authentic understanding. The pre-evangelization of the missioners was brought to a climax. As at Bethlehem when the Son of God became man in Jesus and began the overthrow of the power of the Roman Empire, at Tepeyac Christ entered the soil of the Americas and began the reversal of the European domination of the people of those lands. Tepeyac marks the beginning of the reconquest, and of the birth of Mexican Christianity.

It is from within the poor that the process of conversion is begun. The poor become the heralds of a new humanity. This critical challenge of our compassionate and liberating mother to the powerful of any moment and place in the Americas continues today to be the dynamic voice and power of the poor and oppressed of the Americas groaning and travailing for a more human existence. Her presence is not a pacifier but an energizer which gives meaning, dignity and hope to the peripheral and suffering people of today's societies. Her presence is the new power of the powerless to triumph over the violence of the powerful. In her, differences are assumed and the cathartic process of the cultural-religious encounter of Europe-America began, but it has a long way to go. Nevertheless, it has begun and is in process. This is the continuing miracle of Tepeyac—the mother-queen of the Americas. Now, the dreamed of, prayed for and worked for new Church and New World have definitely begun. The new people of the land would now be the mestizo people—La Raza—and the new Christianity would be neither the cultural expression of Iberian Catholicism nor the mere continuation of the pre-Cortez religions of indigenous America but a new cultural expression of Christianity in the Americas.

Today, theologians cannot afford to ignore the function and meaning of popular religion for the popular masses.[13] A theologian's task is not the canonization or rejection of the religious symbols of the people, but a continuous re-interpretation of them in relation to the whole Gospel. In this way popular religion will not be alienating, but will help to lead people to a deeper knowledge of the saving God. It will not be alienating or enslaving, but salvific and liberating. Popular religion which is regenerated (not eliminated) by the Gospel becomes the invincible and efficacious power of the powerless in their struggle for liberation.[14]

For millions of Mexicans and Mexican Americans of the USA, our Lady of Guadalupe is the temple in whom and through whom Christ's saving presence is continually incarnated in the soil of the Americas and it is through her mediation that:

> He shows strength with his arm
> He scatters the proud in the imagination of their hearts.
> He puts down the mighty from their thrones,
> and exalts the oppressed
> He fills the hungry with good things,
> and the rich he sends away empty handed.
>
> *(Luke 1:51–52)*

Notes

1. For an excellent exposition of this point in relation to the popular religion of Mexico cf: J. Meyer, *La Cristiada* (Mexico, 1974), pp. 316–23.

2. 'Culture' is used here as all those solutions which a group finds in order to survive its natural and social situation. It is the complete world vision— norms, values, and rituals—of a group. Spain and Mexico had very highly-developed cultures at the time of the clash.

3. *Tepeyac* is the hill north of Mexico City where the sanctuary of Tonántzin (which means our Mother)—the female aspect of the deity—was located. It was one of the most sacred pilgrimage sites of the Americas. Cf., B. de Sahagun, *Historia general de las cosas de Nueva España* (Mexico, written in mid 1500s), vol. 3, p. 352.

4. *Mestizo* is the Spanish word for a person who is born from parents of different races. In contemporary Latin America it is acquiring a positive meaning and the arrival of Columbus is celebrated as the day of *La Raza* (The Race), meaning the new race formed of Europe and Native America. There is no English translation of this concept as the English word 'half-breed' (a social rather than a biological term) is very derogatory and would have a completely different meaning.

5. For the first twelve missioners who came to Mexico, 'New World' was a theological term indicating the place where the new Christianity was now to emerge. It would not be simply a continuation of the Christianity of Europe, but a new, evangelical Christianity. See: S. Zavala, *Recuerdo de Vasco de Quiroga* (Mexico, 1965); J. Lafaye, *Quetzalcóatl et Guadalupe* (Paris, 1974), pp. 52–67.

6. Some of the native American cultures were very well-developed and in many ways were superior to those of the Europe of the sixteenth century. For a good description of this, see: M. Leon-Portilla, *Aztec Thought and Culture* (Norman, Oklahoma, 1963), especially chapter 5, pp. 134–176 (*La filosofia Nahuatl*, Mexico, 1974).

7. O. Paz, *The Labyrinth of Solitude* (New York, 1961), pp. 93–96 (*El labertino de la soledad*, Mexico, 1959).

8. Leon-Portilla, *op. cit.*, pp. 74–79.

9. J. Soustelle, *La vie quotidienne des Aztèques à la velle de la conquête espagnole* (Paris, 1955).

10. For a very good description of the development of the Guadalupe tradition, cf. Lafaye, *op. cit.*, pp. 281–396.

11. Leon-Portilla, *op. cit.*, p. 102.

12. For a good example of a scholar who has been able to penetrate the historical consciousness alive in the folklore of the people, see: N. Wachtel, *La vision des vaincus* (Paris, 1971); and R. Acuña, *Occupied America* (San Francisco, California, 1973).

13. Pope Paul VI, *Evangelii Nuntiandi* (December 8, 1975), sections 48 (on popular piety) and 63 (on adaptation and fidelity in expression); see also: Meyer, *op. cit.*, p. 307 brings out the false way in which Mexican Catholicism has been judged by North American and European missioners.

14. Meyer, *op. cit.*, pp. 275–323.

Jean-Marc Ela

Ancestors and Christian Faith:
An African Problem

MY subject here is meaningless for a Christianity which is no more than a transposition of foreign dogmas, rites, rules and customs, and which breaks abruptly with African traditions. But it is a very serious problem for a faith which does not impose itself like a law, but sensitively assumes the characteristics of a culture. It is clear that that kind of openness demands some purification and liberation. In this respect, the famous Chinese Quarrel of the Rites is still a paradigm for the difficulties of a Christianity attached to a particular type of civilization and incapable of freeing itself from contingent structures in order to open itself up to the universal element in present history. In an age in which the idea of catholicity tended to be identified with the purely western idea thereof, the outlook of Ricci and his companions came up against the ethnocentrism of the seventeenth century.

If the past illumines the present, how are we to re-evaluate the Christian message in order to prevent it from being a disturbing influence in an age of acculturation when, faced with a dominant civilization, the African rejects any surrender of his cultural identity? That is certainly the vital context of the question with which I am concerned here. In fact, even if the ancestors are not discredited and accorded a peripheral position, how are we to live and express our faith so that it is not the alienating reflection of a foreign world behaving aggressively towards indigenous customs and beliefs? At a time when, in certain burgeoning communities, the Elders are reproaching young Christians with forgetting the dead, surely we must ask what the Gospel's attitude is to the ancestor cult. The question should be put unflinchingly if we are to pay due attention to the actual existence of each of our African nations

34

with its diversity, fundamental human aspirations and problems: Can the Church in black Africa become the possible location of communion with the ancestors?

AFRICAN SYMBOLISM

We must remember a fact of some importance. It is rare in black Africa for the dead not to be honoured by any cult after the funeral ceremonies, which take place in accordance with the rituals of each ethnic group. In several traditional societies the cult of the dead is perhaps the aspect of a particular culture to which an African feels most attached. It represents a heritage to which he clings despite everything. In fact the ancestor cult is so widespread in Africa that it is impossible to escape the problems that it raises at the level of Christian life and thought. In certain countries it is followed officially. A typical example is Zaïre where, during official receptions, the first glass has to be raised in honour of the ancestors by pouring a few symbolic drops on the ground where they are interred. This homage takes the many forms proper to each African society. To describe all its aspects would be beyond the scope of the present article. In order to go more deeply into the aspect of the problem which is pertinent here, it is enough to study the basic structure of the ancestor cult in black Africa and to try to elicit its deep significance.

In this regard I must emphasize the importance of the signs which invest and enfold the life of the African, and which remind him of the presence of the ancestors in the warp and woof of his life. An important aspect of this process is the value of the new name given during initiation, which constitutes not only a language of gestures and symbols but a decisive experience enclosing an ontological transformation that confers a way of being in the world in regard to the ancestors. We must also remember, in terms of spatial existence, the family cavern where the dead of several generations lie in their tombs. For the African mind, a tomb is the concentrated presence of the invincible: the cemetery where the ancestors lie is a sacred place. It is there that one makes offerings to them and consults them about serious problems. For the Bantus, the most solemn oath is sworn on their tombs. Black art serves the ancestor cult. There is no mistaking the rôle and function of ancestor statues and masks in a large number of African societies. We know nowadays that these objects are not fetishes, as European amateurs of exotic art have long claimed they are. The statue and the mask are important but exist on a human and not a divine level. A statue is not worshipped; it manifests the spiritual presence of the ancestor. The symbols which sometimes appear on the statue of the ancestors declare what the power of each ancestor was. The example of their actions is an encouragement now. It is a stimulus to descendants. Thus a true solidarity is established in time between the generations. In the same sense, it is important to remember the evocative power of the negro mask which 'dramatizes' the presence of the ancestor among the living. In other societies some ethnic groups preserve beneath the ground the ancestor's skull to which libations are regularly offered, as among the Bamleke. Elsewhere the simpler measure is adopted of an altar for parents and grandparents. Among the northern Cameroon highlanders, where the Ancestor cult is very developed, each head of family has a clay figure which represents his father or grandfather.

This clay figure is often called 'Baba', using the same term a man uses for his father when alive. It is surprising to see populations which to all intents and purposes are the most primitive, and from which one would expect very materialist reactions, rising to the level of a spiritualization of this kind: worship, that is, neither of tombs nor of skulls but of a purely symbolic element. In entire highlands of northern Cameroon, the soul of the dead person dwells in an empty jar, which is usually placed below the millet loft, which is the heart of the highlander's home. There the ancestors have their privileged place. If on finding these jars, one asks: 'What is that?' the head of the household answers at once: 'It is my father' or 'It is my grandfather'. Ancestor worship is an appropriate illustration of a major aspect of African symbolism.

No ritual action relating to the ancestors is conceivable without the family group; hence the Mada of northern Cameroon use the term 'pra' to designate both the jar which stands for the ancestor and the 'worship' given to him. In other words, no prayer, libation, sacrifice or celebration of the feast of the ancestors is possible without 'pra'. Hence the basis of ancestor worship is the jar which affirms the existence and presence of the dead. In this instance a symbolic object conditions a dramatization intended to make present the person whom one invokes. Moreover the ancestor cult is already expressed in and by means of the sign which permanently recalls the presence of the ancestor to the conscious minds of the members of the community. But the funeral jar is not only the condition of a liturgy of the dead; it also expresses the African understanding of death.

It is characteristic of many African cultures never to say of someone that he is dead. One always says of a person that he or she has gone away; that he or she has left us; and is no longer here or has passed away. John Mbiti has collected a long list of such expressions from various regions of Africa.[1] For the African, death is not an annihilation of being. Ultimately, there is no fear of death. Anxiety is, however, felt about 'dying' without a child. The absence of boys in particular is the worst curse possible. Yet beyond this obsession with the child we can see a deep concern: the ancestor cult is the main intention behind the desire for heirs. It is a fearsome thing to die if one has broken all links with family, clan and community. More exactly, the African fears 'dying' without leaving behind some who 'will remember him, without leaving behind a community to which he can connect himself'.[2] Without a cult, the dead person is condemned to wander without any form of communication with the living. Hence the importance of the funeral vessel. It is a sign of living communication with the ancestors. Because it makes the presence of the departed actual, it is the primordial sign illuminating the basic African thought: 'The dead are not dead'. The jar is evidence of that nearness of the invisible which is probably the centre of gravity of the African religious universe. It functions therefore as a 'symbol' which brings close and keeps together what appears to be far away. It enables one to overcome the distance and oblivion brought about by death. In short, it is a factor unifying the living and the dead.

Among the pagan populations of northern Cameroon, where this sign is always to be found, the ancestor jar plays a truly hierophantic role. It is a symbol which provides contact with the ancestor by means of a relation of signification. In praying 'to' the 'pra', the Mada speak as if they were addressing a real person. A current of mutuality is established between the being symbolized and the person who enters into contact with him by means of the symbol. Ultimately the 'pra' is a vital knot by means of which the ancestor enters into communication with the living, and is able to exert his influence immediately and directly. To understand the structure of ancestor 'worship', we have to return to the importance of symbolism in African culture. But this structure is inseparable from the total vision of man and society. It exists within the context of kinship which subtends all sectors of traditional African society.[3] Kinship may be defined as a vast operational system organizing individuals within a co-ordinated network of mutual actions and reactions. That is, I think, the basis of all the relations and attitudes which in Africa mediate communion between living and dead.

Kinship brings into play a vision of the world according to which man is made to go beyond earthly restrictions. The main actions of the ancestor cult allow communitarian bonds which defy the gulf of death. In a society within a cosmic and sacred order enfolding everything, the ancestors are remembered in critical moments of individual life and of the entire social group. Birth, marriage, agricultural feasts; all these are integrated into the coherent whole of traditional society in which man, in communion with the powers of nature, is defined in terms of his relationship with God and the ancestors. What justifies reference to the dead in the events which mark the life of the group is the structure of kinship. To understand the fundamental meaning of ancestor 'worship' one has to see it in the African context of the family, which is the basis of culture. Thanks to the kinship system, the ancestors are still connected to their families, and continue to protect the living, to look after them and to act as their intermediaries; at the same time they are open to the interests and worries of the living.

The ancestor 'cult' not only offers communion with the dead but reinforces bonds between the living. Hence the feast of the bull, among the highlanders of northern Cameroon, even though celebrated in honour of the ancestors, has more than a mere sacrificial significance. This expression of the 'cult' also has considerable meaning for social life. When the feast of the ancestors comes round, each area invites 'all the mountain' to take part in the celebrations, thus allowing everyone to visit one another successively in each hamlet. Everyone, young or old, enjoys the same feeling of communion which reinforces the unity and cohesion of the ethnic group. If we do not stress the sacrifice offered, we of course forget a major dimension of the highlanders' life. In the sacrificial meal at which each member of the family receives his share, there occurs that communication and therefore communion of life which interrelates various groups born from a common ancestor. For the highlanders celebrating it, the feast of the bull has a primordial value: it is an institution which illustrates and simultaneously maintains the power of the head of the family and allows belief in the ancestors. Although God usually gets a sheep, the feast in honour of the ancestors requires the sacrifice of a bullock. Ultimately, what is in question is the fundamental communion in which everyone finds his reason for existence and life.

LIVING THE RELATION TO THE DEAD IN CHRIST

Does maintenance of the relationship between living and dead have any place in life in Jesus Christ? In other words, if he is to convert to the Gospel must an African break his relationship with the ancestors?

A preliminary remark is apposite here. The fact that the ancestors have not had any place in the life of African Christians until now resulted from the tendency of missionaries to confound 'ancestors' and 'spirits'. Belief in spirits which was one of the superstitions deemed incompatible with Christian faith. Accordingly, the 'ancestor cult' was seen as a variant of the 'spirit cult', a global term for various forms of animism. In that view, an African wishes to placate the souls of his ancestors so that they do not harm him. The dead are confused with maleficent spirits which have to be appeased by sacrifice. Ultimately the fear of spirits would then be the basis of the ancestor cult.

That interpretation takes into account neither the overall structure of the bonds between the living and the dead, nor the ritual actions which are characteristic of relationship with the ancestors. It is not fear which persuades the Mada of northern Cameroon to cultivate the 'pra' of their fathers, but the need to remain in communion with them and to enable them to participate in various moments of family life. In so far as the veneration of ancestors is integrated into the overall context of a civilization based on millet, it is inconceivable that a head of a household who has inherited his father's fields would prepare the beer with the new millet without making an offering to his father. At any beer meeting, the head of the household always begins by pouring the ancestor's share on the ground. There is a very significant rite in which the highlanders, after presenting the child to the sun (which symbolizes God, the source of life), place the child under the protection of the ancestors. None of these actions is inspired by fear of evil spirits. The 'spirits' theme corresponds in the African context to a symbolism of evil, whereas belief in the ancestors is based on a quite different understanding of existence and the universe. In Africa the 'dead' form part of the family. They do not represent hostile 'powers' whose evil influences have to be neutralized by means of quasi-magical rites. They are not excluded from the events of tribal life but their presence is actually experienced as the participation of the invisible world in the life of the living. Moreover, the libations and food offerings made to the dead are marks of respect and brotherhood in a cultural context in which communication with the invisible is an aspect of the total reality in which man lives. The 'cult' of the ancestors is not synonymous with the 'spirit cult' precisely because the community in its everyday life carries on a form of communication in which those who have passed away, far from having disappeared, continue to subsist as significant elements. In other words, the dead person and—indissolubly—death itself, are integrated with one another in the system of relations which an individual shares with nature, family and society. Hence the food and drink offered to the ancestors are symbols of the continuity of the family and of permanent contact. For the African, these offerings express an attitude that is not destroyed by passage into the realm of the invisible. It is still a question of what was always important: behaving towards an ancestor as if he were alive. The offering of food to a dead father is an action dictated by filial piety.

It would be far too hasty a judgment to characterize as 'pagan', let alone 'idolatrous', what is no more than an 'anthropological reality'. Here I must indicate a serious misunderstanding. In using the words 'cult' or 'worship' in reference to the ancestors, the words do not have the sense they have for many Christians. 'Cult' and 'worship' are terms inappropriate to the African context in which man expresses in a relationship of communion his respect for the founders of the tribe. A family relationship should not be given the title 'cult' in the strict sense of the term. When people offer beer and food to the dead, they are very well aware that they are not worshipping the dead, but are reliving a form of kinship with them, by actualizing it in an existential situation. This action is not 'religious' but a mode of symbolic experience. Mbiti rightly states: 'When these acts concern the dead-who-are-alive, they are a symbol of brotherhood, a recognition of the fact that the dead are still members of their families, and a sign of respect and memory offered to the dead-who-are-alive'.[4] We have to return to the African understanding of death if we are to understand the deep significance of what, for want of a better term, I refer to here as the 'ancestor cult'. But we must also remember the importance of the symbolism. Finally, we have to locate the relationship with the dead-who-are-alive in the kinship system. Hence we must avoid all notion of 'religion' in regard to the ancestor cult. As Anselme Titianma Sanon has remarked: 'for us worship is a dramatic celebration which makes present a spirit or invisible being and which can take place by means of the sacrifice of such animals as chickens or goats. It comprises no idea of adoration or veneration, contrary to what some Christians now think'.[5] If, therefore, relations with the ancestors consist in the belief that the profound communion established between the members of a family is not broken by death but continues in spite of and beyond death, we have to acknowledge that there is nothing in it which is inimical to Christian faith. Does that mean that the highlander of northern Cameroon can keep the jar which represents his father or grandfather, and offer it whatever is prescribed by tradition?

To answer this question we have to recall the Roman decisions on the Chinese rites (December 8, 1939) and on the honour paid to Confucius, on the Japanese rites (May 26, 1936) and the Malabar rites (April 9, 1940). The controversies which arose in regard to those rites have produced explanations of principles and practical rules which are worth attention. In respect of missionary action, the Sacred Congregation of Propaganda affirmed that a cultural phenomenon, even if it is religious in origin, does not constitute a fundamental obstacle to purity of faith, whereas an essentially religious rite may be incompatible with the demands of the Gospel. Therefore it would be wrong to proscribe in the name of faith customs which are characteristic of a civilization and which in fact have nothing to do with religious life. In regard to the Chinese rites and the honours paid to Confucius, Rome made a distinction between actions which are intended to constitute a religious cult and to offer 'honour due to an illustrious person in due respect to ancestral traditions'. More precisely, it is necessary to make a difference between the cult which is the expression of a religion and a 'homage which may be looked on as purely civil'.[6] I have shown above that we cannot consider as 'worship' or 'cultic' the offerings of libations, which are principally marks of filial piety. Those practices which seem to have the characteristics of a cult are, as far as the African is concerned, only a way of translating a kinship relation into symbolic terminology. What is the attitude of the Church to this aspect of African tradition? That is the essential question which belief in ancestors poses for Christian faith. What is in question here is a particular conception of the family. In the course of the famous instruction of Propaganda of 1659, Paul VI, in a 'message to Africa', declared his respect for the traditional values of the black continent. Among those values the pope stressed the 'sense of family' and the 'respect which is shown to the function of, and the authority of, the head of a family', who in certain African civilizations acquires a 'typically priestly function, by virtue of which he acts as a mediator between God and his family'. Is there any reason why an African should not assimilate into his faith in Christ this sense of the family with all its implications and dimensions; for in Africa the invisible is as real as the visible, the two being inseparable and communicating with one another by means of the appropriate symbols?

It is true that in different societies Africans offer sacrifices to their ancestors. This fact implies a killing of the victim which poses a problem for the Christian reader of the Letter to the Hebrews. That also assumes a blood offering, prayer and invocation which vary according to circumstances. Finally there is a communion of the 'noble' parts of the victim. I must add here that a sacrifice is never offered without consulting the soothsayer, whose rôle may be taken in certain ethnic instances by smiths belonging to untouchable castes. Finally we should note that in misfortune, sickness, a poor grain harvest, drought, sterility, a wife leaving, infant death, defeat of some kind, successive deaths in a single family—the soothsayer attributes the events which have occurred to a sin—which generally consists in forgetting the relationship with the dead. Natural mishaps, in short whatever affects the fruitfulness of earth or men, or the health of children, are seen as events which may denote negligence in the carrying out of duties towards the dead. The soothsayer will tell me, for instance, that it is my ancestor-father who is *causing* the sickness of my child, and that he wants food. The soothsayer will ask me to make an offering of food which he prescribes.[7] This overall situation is liable to provoke conflicts between faith and tradition.

We must remember however that one offers a sacrifice of reparation to an ancestor because he has the symbolic features of the father who knows, punishes and rewards. The ancestor's life crystallizes the teachings of the family, of the ethnic group and the culture. In black Africa, the ancestors exercise social control in the true sense, for they are the guardians of tradition. Moreover, in re-establishing the cultural order of relations which the living enjoy with the dead, I am so to speak re-establishing the natural order of things. Belief in ancestors who represent fatherhood plays an essential role in African therapy, according to the ruling idea of the particular sickness.[8] In this context, the sacrifice offered to the ancestor as a token of reparation is never an act of 'adoration'. For the people under consideration here, true religion is sacrifice to God. For although it is deep-rooted in custom, belief in the ancestors does not take the place of a coherent monotheism which obliges us to question the notion of 'animism', a vague though convenient term which has been used for African religions.

God remains the Lord of heaven and earth; and from him, in collective prayer, the elders request the goods of creation and especially that 'freshness' which plays so great a part in the religious thought of the highlanders. The fundamental importance of grain in the life of the populations of the northern Cameroon is underlined by the numerous rites and the major seasonal sacrifices. After the sowing feast, when God is asked to grant rain, there come gleaning and harvest, and then the 'ouzom i Jegla', or 'beer of God', takes place. This is the feast of thanksgiving to God for the new harvest. God is never obscured in favour of the 'power' of the ancestors. Even though ceremonies are organized in honour of the dead of a family, it cannot be said that the worship which ought to be offered to God is offered to the ancestors. The ancestors do not replace the Divinity to whom all things are referred. It is more appropriate to speak of the rôle of mediation played by the heads of families right up to and into the beyond. That is a major characteristic of the African mentality and one which is shown in the smallest things: if one has to pass on a message one does not directly address the person in question, but a third party, even in the presence of the addressee. Not having taken that into account, some observers have supposed that blacks believe in the Deity without according him any 'right of intervention' in daily life, and reserving that right for the ancestors. Apart from the great seasonal sacrifices or a disaster, God is said to be rarely the subject of sacrificial prayers. Periodically, so it is claimed, God is addressed but only under the pressures of everyday life. It is only one step from that thought to the assertion that the 'ancestor cult' is African religion; and it is a step all the more easily taken under the impression that the African God is a remote God who does not intervene in human affairs.

Perhaps the time has come to revise all theories about the place of almighty God in Africa. For the natives of savannah or forest, God is closer to human life than was supposed in the past. And there is no instance in which the ancestors are placed on a divine level in order to justify the worship given them. The sacrifice of reparation offered to the ancestor cannot therefore be considered as a form of idolatry but as the acknowledgment of the authority of the ancestor who in death remains the guarantor of the order of nature and the judge of moral life.

What about the divination which is included along with the sacrifice? Do we have to surrender the sacrifice on account of the practice of divination which seems to be so deep-rooted? We know that the soothsayer has always been persecuted by missionaries. He was for them the very incarnation of African superstitions and of paganism. But the place of the soothsayer in a traditional society demands a more sensitive judgment. As one ethnologist says, divination 'is in fact as the true "overall phenomenon"'. It permits of a practical conception of family or social conflicts and of anxieties and tensions in the religious domain. Moreover, in a spontaneous way it shows what idea people have of the ideal organization of their society while at the same time disclosing their notion of the supernatural'.[9]

If we adopt this global approach, we cannot view the practices of divination as purely religious phenomena. The true question is not therefore one of knowing whether the African should break with his ancestors because he has recourse to soothsayers when he offers sacrifice to the ancestors. It is rather a question of asking how he can live in Christ his relationship with the dead in a universe with its own techniques, theory of knowledge, way of interpreting reality, and system of formalization and explanation. More exactly, how is he to live his faith in a socio-cultural context where everything that happened has a meaning which he is bound to decypher? People see the events of everyday life as having a significance which accords with belief in the ancestors; hence reality has to be 'decoded' on the basis of various signs which manifest that reality. Recognition of 'ancestor worship' in Christian communities in Africa meets with difficulties which have nothing to do with the meaning of the cult but arise from socio-historical obstacles.

CHRISTIAN LIFE AND CHANGES IN AFRICAN SOCIETY

Ethnologists are becoming increasingly aware that it is less and less possible in black Africa to find a society whose functioning is not disturbed by change. What will become tomorrow of the feast of the bull or Maray among the highlanders of northern Cameroon? Belief in the ancestors is threatened by urbanization. How many city-dwellers think that the ancestors help them in their everyday life? On this point there are no longer any reassuring certainties. We may refer in this regard to the results of the survey carried out by Raymond Deniel in Abidjan, capital of the Ivory Coast.[10] There young people are alienated from tradition, or just ignore it. Should they continue to offer sacrifices to the ancestors in order to have rich harvests? Instead harvests might be thought to depend more and more on new cultural methods. How is the traditional cultural patrimony to be maintained in the practice of Christian life in a context of a changing African society? African society is obviously affected by events. Hence there is a movement of destruction and of restructuring. How are the contradictions to be surmounted between the desire to be faithful to the due custom and openness to changes which are turning traditional society upside down? We have to take into account this situation of tension and conflict if we are to work out an approach on the basis of observed fact. Today, even if they feel uprooted, a large number of Africans refuse to live their faith by means of a borrowed humanity. Hence the need to rediscover, within the bosom of Christianity, the African face of man. The basic problem of the ancestors within Christian faith has to do with the African vision of man.

We must look closely at the situation of men who, in societies less brutally and less speedily disturbed by change, are found by the Gospel to be faithful to the ancestor cult. In the two instances above, the Roman decision allows a certain broadmindedness. We must recall the importance of the letter of February 28, 1941 in which the Congregation of Propaganda asks that no list should be drawn up of permitted and forbidden rites for fear of a descent to mere casuistry: 'One must strictly avoid making a list of permitted or forbidden ceremonies, lest one returns to casuistic arguments which will reawaken the disputes of the past in another form'. The declaration asks that there should be no descent 'to the level of specific recommendations made point by point'. Finally, very important, it refers to the ultimate decisions of conscience: 'Priests and laity of good will are free to conduct themselves according to the guidance of conscience in individual cases'. This instruction frees one from scruples which might be provoked by the alien nature of customs proper to non-western societies.

In a declaration of October 17, 1935, the bishops of Madagascar gave the following directives: 'Proscription of customs which assume the dead have power over the living; toleration of marks of respect and acknowledgment; no actual custom is formally proscribed, but all customs should develop in a Christian direction'. These directives allow everyone immense opportunities for the definition of a pastoral strategy corresponding to the problems of a particular environment. There is no question of offering readymade answers here. It is enough to emphasize one point: in black Africa belief in the ancestors is too linked with multiple factors of the traditional form of society for its abandonment to do anything other than trigger off an overall crisis in social structure. To be of the same 'pra' reinforces cohesion with the ethnic group. Moreover, a Christian who abruptly breaks with sacrifice to the ancestor would run the risk of compromising the unity of the tribe. He must therefore take account of the 'others' who do not follow the word of God. In particular, he must respect his lineage chief. He cannot cut himself off abruptly from his brothers in the clan and renounce his bonds of kinship.

When the West is suffering from a profound 'death crisis', inasmuch as death is tending to replace sex as the main taboo, we should think hard about the contribution that might be made to Christianity by communion with the ancestors lived in faith. In certain milieus, cremation is the sign of a society which rejects death or which, when it can no longer avoid it, devalues it. It seems to be a radical means of escaping the cult of cemeteries and the dead. This cult appears to be no more than an archaic survival threatened inevitably with regression along with the primitive attitudes with which it is associated. In the meantime the dead disappear into the flowers.[11] In this context, instead of rebutting our ideas about the ancestors, the Church should surely encourage African Christians to remain in contact with their departed loved ones. Of course not everything is perfect in this relationship. In black Africa the ancestor cult needs the complement of the good news of salvation in Jesus Christ. It is by assimilating it that the Church is able to purify, transfigure and save it.

AN AFRICAN WAY OF CELEBRATING

In this perspective the assumption of communal links with the invisible world is one of the fundamental tasks of that 'African Christianity' Paul VI called for in an important address given at the end of the Symposium of African Bishops in Kampala.[12] But good ideas and logical teachings are not enough. They must be incorporated into theology, catechesis and liturgy. The possibilities offered to the young Churches by the second Vatican Council in the area of liturgical and theological pluralism allow us to attempt fruitful experiments in building a universal Christianity. Why should the northern Cameroon highlander break his 'pra' in order to see it replaced with relics on altars? If the 'pra' is condemned as a superstition which has to be renounced in order to enter the Church, surely the African will find the use of relics just as superstitious. In the highlands the 'pra' of one's father is respected, not the bone of a dead man. Inasmuch as there is no prayer to the ancestors without the object that stands for them, Christians can surely permit the presence of that symbolic object when people meet to remember their ancestors.

The feast of November 2 is far from resolving all the problems posed for African Christians by the veneration of the ancestors. We have to find a kind of celebration of All Souls' Day in our village and local communities where the heads of families converted to the Gospel will have a major rôle to play which is also one that accords with tradition. We must remember that custom also provides for an annual commemoration of the departed; the feast when all heads of highland households prepare the wine for the ancestors. The Christian has to live his life in this context. Surely it would be appropriate for him to celebrate two commemorative feasts a year, one required by the official church calendar and the other one in which he takes part within the framework of traditional life but at the same time by referring that participation to Jesus Christ. Perhaps we should canonize the traditional ritual of commemoration of the departed. Or perhaps we should remain content with a parallel calendar. The question is open. It is probably not enough to multiply the number of masses for the dead to answer all the aspirations of the African spirit and its profound intention of living in communion with the ancestors. We have to take into consideration the bad experiences of the Church above all since the Middle Ages when the cult of the dead tended to overburden the liturgy of the living and risked turning the Mass itself into a profit-and-loss procedure. We have to avoid a state of affairs in which practically all the Masses in a week would be taken up by memorials of this or that dead person, to the point where ordinary liturgical life is made impossible for a modern community. People need a cult which is not conventional but nevertheless more integrated into the family context when it is based on reference to the ancestors felt as a necessity.

A eucharist celebrated thus would express the mystery of the faith by signs which bear the imprint of their environment. Then it would no longer be possible to read readymade prayers. Instead there would be a return to the structure of African prayer with its own unique rhythm. Our eyes would not be fixed on the beyond, while we remain indifferent to the realities of this life. On the contrary, prayer would be truly linked to the whole life of the assembled family. In this incarnate prayer we would rediscover the importance of the ancestor's name. The name would be mentioned not by the celebrant but preferably by the respective heads of families, who would be prepared for this 'ministry' in their small communities. The problem posed here is that of a means of celebrating the mystery of salvation which takes into account the demands of the liturgical renewal and of encounter with the values of non-Christian religion.[13] The necessity and the urgency of this attempt are no longer to be shown in the countries where up to now Christianity has always been connected with cultural expressions modelled down to the last detail on the Roman cult—in which everything that was not Christian or western in origin was considered false and systematically excluded. In this context the problem is posed of celebrating the relationship with the ancestors within the world of the Christian faith.

It is hard to think that in Africa veneration of the saints could replace communion with the ancestors. That would deprive converts of a major dimension of their own culture. Anything that might make an African believe that the saints had become his ancestors and that he must henceforth venerate and pray to the saints would be no more than dangerous mystification. Sooner or later converts would find that ecclesiastical pressures would force them to retract. In rejecting the cult of ancestors the Church forces people to practise it in secret. Even if there is (as Pannet has shown) such a thing as a 'popular Catholicism', the cult of the saints which is certainly an integral part of it (with its calendar, devotions, sanctuaries, pilgrimages, religious and even secular feasts, and iconography) is too marked by the historical experience of Christianity in Europe fully to assume the values of African tradition.

We often meet with a popular cult which has arisen from the depths of the spirit of a particular region of Christianity and which is recognized by the people. It is a form of knowledge which is less a matter of exact hagiographical facts than of the accompanying legends (which are always more or less anachronistic), and above all of the special virtues and power of the saint, and of his or her visual image. Think of the names chosen at baptism: if the character of the protective saint is not usually the determining factor in this choice, there can be no doubt that in most traditional Catholic cultures the celebration of his or her feast-day is a special event for the person who bears the name. At a time when the African is searching for his identity, even if—as the Council of Trent declared—'it is good and useful humbly to invoke the saints . . . to have recourse to their prayers, to their aid, and to their assistance' (twenty-fifth session), the faith of the African would refuse the restrictions of a popular cult far too obviously stamped with a certain age, society and culture. The question is not one of knowing which saint of the Roman calendar to dedicate oneself to; it is a matter of knowing how to locate the ancestors in the mystery of faith.

A NEW LANGUAGE OF THE GOSPEL

What, finally, of the ancestors when we try to find a new way of reading the Gospel, a way organically linked with a community-experience in the process of self-discovery and self-creation? All that we can say in regard to the attitude to be taken to offerings and libations to the ancestors, annual commemorations of the dead, and ways of communication with the departed, depends on this radical question which demands a new examination of the Gospel and of tradition. Vatican II reminded us that 'those who have not yet received the . . . Gospel are also chosen to be the people of God'.[14] In other words, those who have not received the fulness of revelation and of faith are no less part of the Church, in a way which has nothing to do with their visible historicity. Who among those whom we look on as our ancestors died in a state of separation from God? And is there a 'pagan' *kirdi* who has not offered a sacrifice to God in his lifetime? In African tradition, to assume the dignity of an ancestor is to suppose that one has excelled in the practice of virtue throughout one's life. Surely the Church of November 1 was also formed by all those pagan ancestors 'who seek you with a sincere heart' (eucharistic prayer IV) and who have been mysteriously worked on by the grace which, not exclusively linked to the sacraments, has taken effect in their hearts? The Council declared that 'those who are inculpably ignorant of the Gospel of Christ and his Church, nevertheless search for God with a sincere heart and try under the influence of his grace to act so as to accomplish his will as their conscience reveals and dictates it to them, can attain to eternal salvation'.[15] It is impossible wholly to exclude the ancestors from the influence of the Logos who enlightens all men who come into this world. We can place them among those who are Christians 'according to the Logos', of whom St Justin speaks.[16] There can, however, be no serious reflection on their status in the one economy of salvation except in terms not only of the Word but of that which is 'beyond the Word': of the Holy Spirit[17] at work in the universe. In this perspective, faith enables us to see our pagan ancestors among that 'great multitude which no man could number, from every nation, from all tribes and peoples and tongues' (Rev. 7:9). Instead of the Christians of Africa remaining satisfied with the invocation of 'saints' of whom they are sometimes wholly ignorant, on the basis of our experience of communion with the ancestors, we must rethink the mystery of the Church as a total communion with those who, for African tradition, are not gods but mediators of the life and benefits of which God is the sole source. In order to communicate the meaning of the Communion of Saints we have to avoid any exclusive stress on those saints canonized and recognized by the ecclesiastical institution. In our context, we have to put the emphasis on 'all the dead whose faith is known to you alone' (eucharistic prayer IV). A Church which mentions in its official prayer Abel the just, the sacrifice of Abraham and that offered by Melchisedech (see eucharistic prayer I), cannot exclude our ancestors from the commemoration. To live in the African way the mystery of communion in the Christ who recapitulates the visible and invisible (Eph. 1:10) is to assume a living relationship with the ancestors as a dimension of our total faith. The Communion of Saints includes communion with the ancestors.

That has not always been the case, but for purely historical and contingent reasons. Christianity was born in persecution. The first Christians saw their fathers die before their eyes. Many were thrown in prison, where they were tortured. In such circumstances it was difficult to return to the ancestor cult. It was too bound up with idolatry, with paganism, and of course the pagans persecuted believers. The Church therefore relied on its own dead, who were all the more deserving of veneration since they testified to the faith. The context of persecution did not allow Christianity to revalue the cult of the ancestors. Christians became a new family in which the cult of the martyrs was substituted for the cult of the dead. In the West the extinction of the cult of the ancestors kept historical pace with the development of the veneration of saints in the Church and the laicization of society. Nowadays November 2 is perhaps no more than an expression of the anxiety of western Christianity in the face of death. Of the ancient cult of the dead no more remains than the flowers on graves and the wreath on the tomb of the unknown warrior.

What sort of man does western Christianity want to reproduce in Africa? Does the Gospel help us really to be ourselves? What is left over for the African as such if he has to give up living in relation to his ancestors? What kind of man does God want to make of us on the basis of the specifically African countenance of man? Surely communion with the ancestors is a mark of our culture. At a time when the Church is opening up to the human and spiritual values of non-European civilizations, Africa questions the Christianity of the origins, not in order to organize a readymade faith and cult, but gradually to produce a new language of the Gospel on the basis of the life of peoples whose belief in the ancestors is a deep-rooted experience.

Translated by John Maxwell

Notes

1. J. Mbiti, *Religions et Philosophie africaine* (Yaoundé, 1972), pp. 162 ff.

2. J. Mbiti, *op. cit.*, p. 168.

3. On the function of kinship in Africa, see D. Paulme, 'La notion de la parenté dans les sociétés africaines', in *Cahiers Internationaux de Sociologie*, XV, 1953.

4. J. Mbiti, *op. cit.*, p. 70.

5. A. T. Sanon, *Tierce Eglise ma Mère, ou la conversion d'une communauté paienne au Christ* (Paris, 1972), p. 246.

6. See *Le Siège apostolique et les missions*, II, p. 154.

7. For the details, see J. F. Vincent, 'Divination et Possession chez les Mofu, montagnards du Nord-Cameroun', in *Journal de la Société des Africanistes*, XLI, 1 (1971), pp. 118 ff.

8. Cf. M. Hebga, *Croyance et guérison* (Yaoundé, 1973).

9. J. F. Vincent, *op. cit.*, p. 71.

10. R. Deniel, *Religions dans la ville. Croyances et changements sociaux à Abidjan* (Abidjan, 1975), pp. 76–77.

11. See P. Ariès, 'La mort inversée. Le changement des attitudes devant la mort dans les sociétés occidentales', in *Maison-Dieu*, no. 101 (1970), pp. 57–89.

12. Cf. *Documentations catholiques*, September 1969, no. 1546, col. 765.

13. I am thinking mainly of the constitution on the liturgy (art. 37) and of the decree on non-Christian religions.

14. *Lumen Gentium* (art. 16).

15. *Ibid.*

16. Justin, 1 *Apol.* 46.

17. See Hans Urs von Balthasar, 'Le Saint-Esprit, l'inconnu au-delà du Verbe', in *Lumière et Vie*, no. 67 (1964).

Leslie Desmangles

Baptismal Rites: Religious Symbiosis of Vodun and Catholicism in Haiti

ANYONE who has either read about Haiti or has visited it has heard the popular maxim that most Haitians are a hundred per cent Roman Catholic and ninety-nine per cent Vodunist. These words capture one of the central paradoxes of Haitian culture. Catholicism is a religion which allows the Haitian peasant to find a place in the official structure of his country; Vodun, on the other hand, provides a means through which he can cope with the problems of his personal life, and those of his daily existence.

The Haitian peasant finds it logical that he must be Catholic 'to serve' the Vodun gods (*loas*), for he sees Catholicism and Vodun as necessary aspects of his existence. He recognizes that the world is governed by dual cosmological forces, represented by the God and saints of the church on the one hand, and by the *loas* of Vodun on the other. For him, the priest in his celebration of the Mass functions as a point of contact with an impersonal Godhead who rules the universe. By contrast the Vodun priest (*houngan*), in his performance of the Vodun ceremony, establishes contact with the minor deities. Hence the Haitian peasant gives his loyalty to both religions in parallel ways. As a good Catholic, he confesses regularly, receives Communion once a year and participates in one pilgrimage annually, parading in the streets of Haitian towns and cities. But his observance of the rituals of the Church does not signify his total acquiescence in its doctrines. He is equally devoted to the Vodun temple (*hounfort*). There, he pays his fees to the *houngan*, consults him about the practical problems of his daily life, and participates annually in one pilgrimage sponsored by the *hounfort*. In short, the Vodunist practices two religions simultaneously.

The prominence of Catholic practices in the Haitian peasant's life today marks the success of the Catholic missionaries who went to Haiti during the colonial period. For these early missionaries went forth, longing to re-enact the miracle of Pentecost and to reach all men regardless of their race. They believed that in Christ there was to be 'no Jew, nor Greek, neither free, nor slave' (Gal 3:28). Filled with this sense of evangelical obligation, the Haitian Church worked zealously, setting in motion a series of events which were to leave their mark on Haitian culture. Vodun meetings among the slaves were outlawed. Magical and religious practices connected with Africa were made crimes; and offenders were punished by torture or by death. The severity of such laws as the *Code Noir* (1685), which ordered all masters to have their slaves instructed and baptized in the "Catholic religion, Apostolic and Roman" within eight days after their arrival in the New World,[1] drove African rituals underground, and necessitated the still nocturnal character of Vodun.

The hostility of the Catholic clergy towards Vodun caused the slaves to mask their African religious traditions behind a *façade* of Catholic practices. Catholicism and African religions made contact in Haiti during the colonial period, and set in motion a process of religious acculturation. In this process, the slaves did not abandon their African religious practices but added to them elements of the Catholic rituals. This subterfuge did not go unnoticed by the missionaries. As early as 1724, Père Labat observed that 'Vodun' assemblies often intermixed sacred things of one religion with objects of an idolatrous cult:[2]

> The negroes [sic] . . . secretly keep all the superstitions of their ancient idolatrous cult with the ceremonies of the Christian religion. All the negroes have much devotion for the communion wafer. They eat it, only when they are ill, or when they are afraid of some danger. In regards to the blessed water the little bit that is consecrated during the Sunday mass, it is rare that one finds one drop of it when the ceremony has ended; they carry it in little calabashes and drink some drops when they rise (in the morning) in pretending that it will guarantee their welfare against all the witchcraft that might befall them.[3]

Père Labat's comments seem to suggest that the slaves did not genuinely embrace Christianity but paid lip-service to it. They adopted Christianity as a veneer, what Jean Price-Mars called a 'Christianisme d'apparat' behind which they practiced their African 'superstitions'.[4] Behind the *façade* of Christian practices, the slaves maintained cultural and religious continuity with Africa. The nocturnal Vodun meeting provided a communal spirit and a basis for a sense of identity, an identity that created an inward freedom by which the slaves could withstand the oppressive conditions of slave labour.

Even after Haiti became independent of France in 1804, the Roman clergy expressed embarrassment about the encroachment of what they called 'heathen practices' on their theology. Because Vodun's spread was so extensive, it is not surprising that throughout Haiti's history, the Catholic Church has campaigned intensely to eradicate 'fetishism' from the island. Thus in 1860, 1896, 1913, 1939 and 1941 the Church renewed its efforts by leading 'antisuperstitious campaigns' which destroyed and burned Vodun temples throughout the nation.[5]

In Haiti today, the Vodunist's allegiance to two religions has the same communal function it had during the colonial period. Like his slave forbears, the Vodunist cannot be a 'single-minded' Catholic. To establish a spiritual identity with his community, he uses his public observance of the Catholic rituals as a veil for his African religious ties. Dorsainvil says that the life of the Haitian peasant is marked by a 'war of nerves'. Although Dorsainvil, a psychiatrist, is referring to the poor nutritional habits of the peasant, his life in the tropics, and his Vodun dances with their frenzy of possession, the statement aptly describes the peasant's religious life as well.[6] Since the Vodunist practices two religions whose doctrines often contradict one another, he is forced to seek correspondences between Catholicism and Vodun in order to deal with these contradictions. By trying to make those correspondences between two religious traditions, he has recreated elements of the church rituals in his Vodun ceremonies. By sticking chromolithographs of saints on the walls of his *hounfort*, by using Catholic rosaries, crucifixes, and candles, he recreates an environment resembling the church sanctuary. By such re-creation, he seeks to reduce the frustrations caused by the intransigent hostility the clergy have so often shown him in the past.

The presence and use of ritual objects from the church in Vodun ceremonies have caused scholarly writers on Vodun to describe it as a syncretism, by which they mean the fusion of traditional African beliefs with Catholic theology. But a close look at the Vodun rituals suggests that the relationship between Vodun and Catholicism is not a syncretism but a symbiosis.[7] I use the word 'symbiosis' here in its etymological and ethnological denotations. Etymologically, symbiosis from *syn* means 'with' (together with) and *bios* means 'life'. In its ethnological context, symbiosis corresponds to what Roger Bastide calls 'syncretism in mosaic'[8]: the juxtaposition or commensalism of two religious traditions which do not fuse with one another.

This juxtaposition or symbiosis can be seen in the Vodun rituals where elements of the Catholic Mass and African rituals coexist. The tiny parts of a stained-glass window are juxtaposed to form a whole; similarly, parts of the African and the Catholic rituals constitute the Vodun ritual. This juxtaposition takes two forms:

First, symbiosis can be seen in the content of the *hounfort* where the rituals are performed. When one stands before a Vodun altar (*pé*), all distance between Vodun and Catholicism seems to be abolished. Votive candles, rosaries, and chromolithographs of saints appear there with sacred rattles, drums, and jars containing the spirits of ancestors.

Second, the priestly hierarchy of the *hounfort* demonstrates this symbiosis, for this hierarchy includes not only the *houngan* and his assistants but a figure known as the *prêt' savanne* (bush-priest), who recites Catholic prayers and fragments of Christian liturgy during various Vodun ceremonies.

The origins of the *prêt' savanne* in Haiti's history are not clear, but his rôle in Vodun was defined in the first years after independence. The first Haitian presidents were friendly to the Church and sought to make Catholicism a state religion with the president as its head.[9] In response, Rome not only refused to recognize Haiti as a black republic, but did not sanction the rôle of the president as the head of the Church. As a result, Haiti entered a period of schism with Rome, and for fifty-six years (1804–60), the Church maintained no seminaries, missionaries or dignitaries in Haiti. James Leyburn reports that under King Christophe in 1814, there were only three Catholic priests in the north of Haiti, one of whom had been appointed archbishop by the state.[10] With few Catholic priests, the early presidents were forced to appoint young priests to ecclesiastical offices; many of them had been slaves, and others 'freebooting' South American exiles who knew just enough of the liturgy to be given charge of a local church. Because these men did not have the evangelical spirit of the early missionaries, many of them willingly occupied an official position in the hierarchy of the *hounfort*. They went to Vodun ceremonies, 'baptizing' houses, doorposts, amulets, and whatever they were paid to do.[11]

From 1804 to 1860, the *prêt' savannes* flourished in Haiti. It was not until 1860, the year of the signing of the *Concordat*, a document which re-established relations between Rome and Haiti, that missionaries returned to the island and the *prêt' savannes* were disbanded. Some who continued their pseudoclerical work were arrested and jailed; others hid from the Church in the *hounfort* where they continued their service to the devotees.

Today the *prêt' savanne* is a part of the hierarchy of the *hounfort*. Although his presence is necessary for the performance of certain rituals in some *hounforts*, he has no independent power. In fact, his rôle is perfunctory. Vodunists see him as a representative of the Church and hence a symbol of its sanction on their Vodun rituals. He is the symbolic embodiment of the contact between the Church and the *hounfort*. Although present at both rituals, he is active only in those of Vodun, yet is central to neither. I shall now examine the rôle of the *prêt' savanne*, focusing especially on the nature of the Vodun rites of initiation, and the function of his rôle in those rites.

VODUN RITES OF INITIATION

Before turning to the rôle of the *prêt' savanne*, we must first examine the symbology of some of the rites of initiation in which he functions.

When a *hounfort* is constructed, the edifice and miscellaneous objects within it are purified and consecrated to the *loas*. By their initiation, a *hounfort* and ritual substances are infused with divine power and thus become the physical residences of the *loas*. Henceforth, the substances will be the doors through which communication can be established between the community of men and the world of the *loas*.

Like edifices and ritual objects, Vodunists who have been initiated into the service of the *loas* can be possessed by them. Through the medium of their voices and their bodies the *loas* can reveal their will and power to the community of men. The initiation of Vodunists is an ordeal which requires the neophytes to submit themselves to physically painful sacrifices throughout a long training period. Devotees courageous enough to endure the painful stages of this adventure receive certain 'graduated' degrees as members of a local *hounfort* whereby they achieve a closer relationship not only with the *loas* but with the community of men as well.

Graduated degrees in the Vodun rites of initiation remind the observer of West African religions. Like the West Africans, Vodunists give the initiate a new name at the moment of his consecration. Whether applied to a person, a ritual object or an edifice, the name is a name of the deity to whom a person or substance is sanctified. Names are of such vital importance to these rites that no ceremony can take place until a name has been ascribed to each substance to be consecrated.

The importance of the name lies in its denotation. Because, both in Haiti and in West Africa, the power of the *loas* is believed to reside in their names, affixing a name of a *loa* to persons or substances has the purpose of infusing the power of the *loa* into them. His sacred name is not a mere word but becomes part of the personal property of the bearer, property which must be protected and whose use is exclusively reserved to him. The name functions as a proxy to its bearer; hence, to pronounce it is to call not only the person into being, but his very self, the divine essence with which he is undissoluably linked.

The sacred name given to a person is what makes him an individual. It represents a metamorphosis in his state of being. In West Africa, as in Haiti, mythology conceives of a man not as something fixed and unchanging, but as something in flux, whose being passes through many phases, each phase being reflected by changes in his sacred name. At birth, a man receives a name. At puberty, he receives another because the initiation rites which accompany his consecration mark his rebirth; he ceases to be a child and becomes an adult.

A person's names not only mark the stages of development of his personality, but protect him against impending danger. He escapes it by taking a different self, whose form makes him unrecognizable. In this sense, the close connexion of his name to that of a deity reflects the source of power through which he can draw the divine substance necessary for such protection. Like the Ewe people of Dahomey, Vodunists give children, especially those whose elder brothers and sisters have died young, a name with a frightful connotation in order to protect them from death. They believe that death will be frightened away or deceived, and will pass them as though they were not human at all.[12]

Not only in naming do the Vodun rites of initiation reflect the survival of West African religions, but in their use of water as well. In Haiti, water is used to purify persons or substances in preparing them to embody the *loas*. In parts of West Africa, water is the symbol of purification whereby neophytes, shrines, temples and ritual objects are washed and cleansed of their impurities before they can be consecrated to a deity. The Ewe people of Dahomey, for example, believe that their priests are 'called' by God and that before someone becomes a priest, he is trained first, and then undergoes the ritual ceremonies of initiation involving the pouring of libations to God and to the ancestors, after which the head of the novitiate is washed, cleansed and consecrated before he can undertake his priestly duties.[13] A similar ceremony is performed during the Vodun initiation rites. A vital part of the ceremony, known as *laver tête* consecrates the novitiate to the service of the *loas* in the *hounfort*.

Because these rites include the use of water, Vodunists refer to them as baptisms. Although the term 'baptism' itself is borrowed from Catholicism (the inclusion of it in Vodun's religious vocabulary probably dates from the Haitian colonial period), Vodun interprets the rite differently from Catholicism. Although most Vodunists would agree with Catholics that baptism is a rite of purification which introduces the initiates into the sacred community, there is a further meaning in the rite. For Vodunists, baptism also implies infusing a substance with divine essence so that it becomes a vessel in which a *loa* resides. Vodunists believe that the baptized substance is so thoroughly imbued with the power of the *loa* that at some point during these ceremonies the *loa* leaves his sacred abode to come to the *hounfort* not only to baptize the substance himself, but to enter it.

Having set forth the symbology of Vodun baptisms, we can now turn to the rôle of the *prêt' savanne*. An examination of Vodun baptism is important in studying the symbiosis of Roman Catholicism and Vodun, for in no other ritual are the rites of the church so intermixed with the elements of African religion. In no other Vodun rituals are outward appearances so deceptive. To the untrained eye, Vodun baptism might seem to replay the church's baptismal rites cast in an African setting; and one could easily mistake it for a fusion of Catholic and Vodun practices. But the trained observer sees them differently. What deceives the casual observer is the apparent function of the *prêt' savanne* who, as a tangential member of the temple hierarchy, reads the prayers of the church 'from the book' and chants canticles of the church; he also sprinkles the person or substance being baptized with holy water.

A closer examination of the *prêt' savanne's* presence in numerous Vodun baptisms reveals that his role in them is perfunctory. First, while the *prêt' savanne* recites the prayers of the church, the *houngan* simultaneously performs the Vodun ritual, often rendering many of the *prêt' savanne's* prayers inaudible to the devotees. Second, the *houngan* has power to summon the *loas* to manifest themselves in the *hounfort*; the *prêt' savanne* does not. Third, whenever the *loas* manifest themselves in the ceremony in the body of a possessed devotee, they pay homage to the *houngan* with special salutations due to one whose sacred powers have earned him that right. In contrast, the *loas* offer no salutation to the *prêt' savanne*. Fourth, although the *prêt' savanne* intermittently sprinkles holy water as if baptizing the initiates, the *houngan* carries out the actual baptism and, at the appropriate moment, ritually washes the objects or the heads of persons being sanctified.[14]

Perhaps the best evidence of the limited significance of the *prêt' savanne* is that he is largely a phenomenon of urban *hounforts*. In the remote mountains of Haiti, where there are few churches and where Catholic influence is minimal, the *prêt' savanne* is virtually unknown. For example, in baptismal ceremonies observed in the remote sections of Furcy, there were no instances of recitation of Catholic prayers, or of singing of Catholic canticles. The only part of the rituals which resembled the Catholic ritual was the sprinkling of water on initiates by the *houngan*. The actual baptism did not, however, occur at the moment that water was sprinkled, but later in the ceremony when the *houngan* announced to the devotees that he was proceeding with the ritual of consecration itself. After the ceremony, when questioned about the *prêt' savanne*, the *houngan* was unaware of the significance of the term. Even after I explained the role of the *prêt' savanne* to him, he was uncertain of how the *prêt' savanne* would function in the ritual and appeared embarrassed by what he felt to be his ignorance. Numerous interviews with other *houngans* in Furcy about the rôle of the *prêt' savanne* revealed that they had no need for his services since they had their own way of dealing with the *loas*.[15]

The urban *hounforts* show more clearly the symbiosis of Vodun and Catholicism. There, *prêt' savannes* and *houngans* go about their business simultaneously. The men themselves and the rituals they perform are juxtaposed in space and time. But in the eyes of Vodunists, the work of the *houngan* is important whereas that of the *prêt' savanne* is not. Yet the same Vodunists sense, without understanding why and without seeking to know, that both belong there together, and that the presence of the *prêt' savanne* somehow completes the ceremony.

That the *prêt' savanne's* rôle in the Vodun baptism is indeed tangential seems clear from the following considerations. First, if the rituals of the church and Vodun were really fused, the *prêt' savanne* would have a significant rôle in the actual baptism and would perform some efficacious act of baptism separately from the *houngan*. Second, if the rôle of the *prêt' savanne* were necessary in these rituals, the *loas* would salute him when they manifest themselves in the ceremonies through the body of a possessed devotee. Third, if he were essential to the baptismal rites, his presence would be necessary in all such ceremonies throughout the country. Finally, if his rôle had been of consequence, his service as an officiant would receive a concomitant response from the *houngan* who performed the rites.

Because the Church does not approve of Vodun and has attempted so often in the past to suppress it, Vodunists feel the need for some symbol of the Church's sanction of their activities in order to identify with the country's official Catholic society. In their effort to imply the approval of the Church, Vodunists have attempted to provide within the structure of their rituals what they consider as desirable in Catholicism. On the one hand, for historical reasons which have caused the persistence of African religion in Haiti, Vodunists have not been able to abandon that heritage—a value symbolized by the rôle of the *houngan* in the community. On the other hand, the magnificence of the Church as reflected in its liturgy and in its sacerdotal vestments has taught them to admire Catholicism as well— an admiration symbolized by the rôle of the *prêt' savanne* in these rituals.

The *prêt' savanne* is, therefore, a symbol of the Church in the baptismal rites. His place in the urban *hounfort* is guaranteed by his ability to bring to the baptismal rites elements of a 'competing' religious system which the *houngan* operating under the framework of African tradition cannot provide, but which nevertheless many Vodunists feel are necessary.

In spite of this analogy, however, the *prêt' savanne* and the *houngan* are not homologous. His prestige among Vodunists is not as great as the *houngan's*. His function has placed him between the *houngan* and the Catholic priest. Vodunists regard him as a supernumerary in the baptismal rites in the *hounfort*. Moreover, Vodunists distinguish between a baptism performed by a Catholic priest and the sprinkling of water by a *prêt' savanne*. One distinction they draw is that a Catholic priest must always be white and the *prêt' savanne* black. Even in their view of the clergy, Vodunists feel that they cannot respect a black Catholic priest. Since the days of the colony, most Catholic priests have been white, and the old tradition lingers in the minds of Vodunists that, much like the water sprinkled on initiates by the *prêt' savanne*, 'Christian baptism will not stick'.[16] Vodunists say that in baptism the Christian God and saints need the intercession of the white priest, but in the Vodun baptism the *loas* need to be summoned by a native *houngan*.[17]

CONCLUSION

By piecing together the details of Vodun baptisms, one can make several observations:

First, the theological concepts behind the Vodun baptismal rites are essentially West African. Although they borrowed the term *baptism* from Catholicism, Vodunists, like some West Africans, connote by it a means whereby a divine essence is infused in a person, an edifice, or an object.

Second, by and large, as rituals Vodun baptisms have retained their African forms. Through ritual washing, the baptized substance becomes a channel through which the *houngan* can draw divine energy into the world of men. The name of that substance which embodies the *loa* is the door through which the divinity can be reached. The key to that door is the utterance of that name.

Third, unlike Catholicism whose ceremonial objects retain their sacredness unless it is removed by special ceremonies of 'degradation', the sacredness of Vodun objects is limited to the religious act which accompanies their use; and, since action is transitory, the power of a divinity comes and goes according to the instances when an object is handled. Maya Deren is therefore right in assuming that Vodun has 'a quality which can be described as a constant "disappearingness"',[18] for when the sacred function of an object is fulfilled, it ceases to be sacred. Hence, a *hounfort* which, during a ceremony, vibrates with the power of the *loas*, the morning after becomes a place where chickens and dogs wander about. Women also sit there to gossip, giving no attention to the presence of the *loa* to whom the entire *hounfort* and its contents are dedicated.[19]

Fourth, the role of the *prêt' savanne* during the baptismal ceremonies is perfunctory. Not only are his prayers inaudible to the devotees, but the actual ritual washing which infuses the power of the *loa* in the substance or the person being baptized is performed solely by the *houngan*. Moreover, the *prêt' savanne* is part of the *hounfort's* hierarchy largely in areas where a Catholic church is present and where it influences the life of the members of the community. In such areas, symbiosis between Catholicism and Vodun takes two forms. First, the presence of the *hounfort* near a Catholic church accomplishes the spatial juxtaposition of Catholicism and Vodun. Second, the elements of the Catholic rites such as the sprinkling of water, and the prayers and canticles chanted by the *prêt' savanne* show the symbiosis of the two religions.

Notes

1. Père Adolphe Cabon, *Notes sur l'Histoire, religieuse d'Haiti, de la Révolution au Concordat 1789–1860* (Paris, 1920, pp. 33ff.

2. 'Vodun assemblés mêloient (*sic*) souvent les choses saintes de notre religion à des objets d'un culte idolâtre'. Père Jean-Baptiste Labat, *Nouveau Voyage aux Isles de l'Amérique*, IV (Paris, 1722), p. 153.

3. 'Les nègres (*sic*) . . . conservent secrètement toutes les superstitions de leur ancien idolâtre avec les cérémonies de la religion chrétienne. Tous les nègres (*sic*) ont une devotion très grande et une foi très vive pour le pain bénit. Ils en mangent, lorsqu'ils se trouvent mal, ou quand ils craignent quelque danger. A l'égard de l'eau bénite quelque quantité qu'on en fasse le dimanche à la grand'-messe, il est rare qu'on en trouve une goutte quand le service est finit; ils l'emportent dans de petites calebasses et en boivent quelques gouttes en se levant et prétendent se garantir par ce moyen de tous les maléfices qu'on pourrait jeter sur eux'.

4. Jean Price-Mars, *Ainsi parla l'Oncle* (Port-au-Prince, 1928), pp. 44–45.

5. Frank Durant, *Cent Ans de Concordat: Bilan de Faillite 1860–1960* (Port-au-Prince, 1960). The daily events which took place during the last campaigns can be found in the Catholic newspaper. See articles by Père J. Foisset, *La Phalange*, 1938–1944.

6. J. C. Dorsainvil, *Vodou et Névrose* (Port-au-Prince, 1934), p. 60.

7. This term has a different meaning in this paper from that usual in the biological sciences, where it refers to the intimate living together of dissimilar organisms in a mutually beneficial relationship. For further discussion of symbiosis in Vodun, see L. G. Desmangles, *God in Haitian Vodun: A Case in Cultural Symbiosis*, Ph.D. Dissertation (Philadelphia, Temple University, 1975).

8. Roger Bastide, *Les Amériques noires* (Paris, 1967) (Eng. trans.: *African Civilisations in the New World* [New York, 1971]).

9. James Leyburn, *The Haitian People* (New Haven, 1941), p. 118.

10. *Ibid.*, p. 121.

11. *Ibid.*, p. 123.

12. J. Spieth, *Der Religion der Ewer* (Leipzig, 1911), p. 230.

13. John S. Mbiti, *Concepts of God in Africa* (Garden City, New York, 1969), p. 221.

14. Information gathered in field research in Haiti, 1974.

15. *Ibid.*

16. Leyburn, *op. cit.*, p. 129.

17. Information gathered in field research in Haiti, 1974.

18. Maya Deren, *Divine Horsemen: The Voodoo Gods in Haiti* (New York, 1970), p. 187.

19. *Ibid.*

Anscar Chupungco

Filipino Culture and Christian Liturgy

CULTURE, OFFICIAL WORSHIP AND LITURGICAL REFORM

HISTORICAL circumstances of the sixteenth and seventeenth centuries conspired against the adaptation of the Roman rite to Filipino culture. In 1563 the Council of Trent entrusted the regulation of the liturgy to the pope alone, and in 1588 Sixtus V established the Congregation of Rites which put an end to the free development of the liturgy in local churches. Missionaries from Spain entered the Philippines with the ideals of Catholic unity which in those days meant, in practice, uniformity with the Roman Church. But a circumstance with more immediate impact on the missionaries was the Chinese rites controversy which beset the Church in far-eastern Asia for over a hundred years after the death of Matteo Ricci in 1610. This controversy created a climate of reserve, not to say hostility, to indigenous rituals and traditions. Under such circumstances to alter anything in the Roman rite on behalf of indigenous culture was inconceivable. Thus, during the formative years of the Church in the Philippines, years which normally would have been ideal for indigenization, no effort was made to integrate the official worship of the Church into Filipino culture. From the liturgical viewpoint the young Church was not a mission Church which enjoyed the privilege of developing its form of worship, by either adopting more suitable forms from other Christian Churches (as Gregory I instructed Augustine to do for England) or borrowing elements from the customs and traditions of the people (as Vatican II's Decree on the Missionary Activity of the Church, art. 22, envisages). From the very outset the missionaries jealously guarded Christian worship against any contact with Filipino animism. Missionaries from Manila who saw the Jesuit experiment in China were shocked at the acts of obeisance performed by Christian converts before the coffins of the recently deceased and before the ancestral tablets. Such acts, they declared, were idolatrous and superstitious. But in spite of the Church's campaign against animism, it took a long time before Filipinos abandoned it. Until the end of the seventeenth century the missionaries were still on the look-out for clandestine animistic rituals which were being performed by church-goers in the forests. In fact, the practice of sprinkling the foundation of a house with the blood of a chicken is a remnant of animism which lingers on in metropolitan Manila. But more crucial to the question of fostering closer contact with the indigenous culture is language. Again the ill-fated Chinese experiment and the initial mistake of Francis Xavier in Japan—by using the Japanese word for God he found himself sponsoring the cause of a Buddhist deity—must have made the missionaries in the Philippines wary of adapting native words to Christian usage. Thus, Spanish words like *Dios, gracia* and *santo* were foisted on the natives and were gradually assimilated by most of the Filipino languages. But culture had its revenge: in the course of time some of these words have assumed meanings which are quite distinct from the original. Rice, for example, is often referred to as the *gracia* of God.

Thus, Christian worship was practically sealed up against cultural intrusions. This explains why after four hundred years it is still foreign to many Filipinos. For these 'new gentiles', unlike the Greco-Romans of the early Church, have not had the chance to assimilate and express the original Christian message of the liturgy in their own thought and language pattern. Whereas the Franco-Germanic peoples adapted the Roman rite to their culture, the Philippine missionaries, inhibited by historical factors, made no effort to adapt it to the Filipino culture. Thus, the Roman liturgy, even in the vernacular, still speaks to God and about God in words which originated from the Greco-Roman culture; in words, therefore, which do not reflect the mind and heart of Filipinos.

Foreign, however, does not mean alienated. The natives not only submitted themselves to the new form of worship brought by the colonizers; they also claimed it as an integral part of their life. Culturally it was and still is an extraneous element in their religious and social experience, yet in a real sense it has become part and parcel of Filipino cultural heritage, a way of life and a social imperative. To be a Filipino Christian meant to be baptized, to 'receive' the sacraments and to 'assist' at Sunday Mass according to the rites of the Roman Church. Indeed, before the advent of Vatican II it was a source of consolation to devout Filipinos to realize that the Mass they attended did not differ much from the Mass celebrated by the pope himself. They understood little or nothing of its ceremonies and language, but through them they experienced a sense of belonging to the Roman Church. It was not without a tinge of fanaticism that Catholics addressed themselves *romano*. The presence of the Roman form of worship in Filipino culture is therefore not a matter of tolerance but of acceptance. At the root of this are devotion to the Roman Church and the hospitality and openness of Filipino culture.

But it is not correct to say that the Roman liturgy had no contact whatsoever with Filipino culture. Given the circumstances of the time, there was nothing that could be done in the realm of the official texts and rubrics, but there was an opening which offered culture the possibility to assert itself and to imprint its character on the liturgy. This opening was the cultural climate in the Church during the seventeenth century. Coming out of the 'autumn of the Middle Ages' and the crisis of Protestant Reformation, the Church was in a mood for celebration. It was the age of the baroque and a felicitous moment for the missionary activity of the Church in the Philippines. For in many ways Filipino culture closely resembles that of the baroque. Indeed, it has been described as a culture of *fiesta*, of festivity and of dramatic and colorful celebrations. This happy coincidence accounts not only for the ready acceptance of the new religion but for its eventual acculturation. It was here that the Filipino genius for synthesizing foreign and native cultural forms was at its best. Churches were built in every principal town in the style of Spanish baroque, but at a glance one can note the Filipino version of the baroque—more playful, exuberant and spontaneous than its archetype in architectural style. One can also note some of the most unexpected variations, often not without a sense of humour, which Filipino artists added to traditional sacred art—the Holy Spirit represented as a dove with wings folded together as if in prayer, the Jewish high priest wearing a pince-nez, or a Chinese merchant in the depths of hell. But it was in the solemn celebration of the Mass before Vatican II's liturgical reforms that one witnessed the flowering of Filipino baroque religiosity. An hour before the Mass a band of musicians went around the town to invite the people to church. During the Mass an amateur chamber orchestra accompanied the polyphonic choir, and at the consecration the elevation of the host was hailed by fireworks, church-bells and the jubilant playing of an anthem.

After more than a decade of liturgical reform one can ask whether the road it has taken in matters involving the rite is suited to the Filipino temperament. Simplification of rites, return to a more austere form of celebration, avoidance of anything dramatic and colourful, and the reduction of liturgical paraphernalia to the minimum—does not all this widen still more the gap between the liturgy and indigenous culture? Already the more creative are finding ways and means to revive the festive mood of the liturgical celebration by introducing the *rondalla* band to accompany the singing or by encouraging a sumptuous display of fresh fruits and cooked food at the offertory procession. One may not, of course, go to excesses in the name of festivity to the detriment of the interiority of Christian worship. Nor may one even harbour the thought of returning to a baroque liturgy which disregards active and intelligent participation, magnifies the external and dwarfs the essential. On the other hand, may one stress the spirituality of worship at the expense of the totality of human experience? In trying to restore the Roman liturgy to its original 'noble simplicity', Vatican II practically abandoned the baroque culture and, for good or ill, left something of a vacuum in the religious experience of Filipinos—for good or ill, because it can either bring about a purifying effect on popular religiosity or alienate the liturgy from native cultural forms. To make things worse, the use of the vernacular has underlined the disarming fact that the translation of Latin texts has not improved liturgical communication. It begins to dawn on many, with something of a shock, that the language of the Roman liturgy is utterly foreign to the *linguaggio* of Filipinos who, as a consequence, cannot identify their form of worship as an authentic expression of their cultural values and aspirations.

These observations are not meant to cast any doubt on the validity of Vatican II's liturgical reform nor to strike a note of gloom on its future in the Philippines. Indeed, the flourishing of parish liturgical life and the active involvement of the laity are giant steps made by the Church after the Council. However, the most profound values of Filipino culture still escape the language and ritual of the reformed Roman liturgy. Although Filipino Christians are deeply imbued with Christian catechetical truths and moral imperatives, and claim to be *romano*, a whole section of their native thought and language pattern is nowhere reflected in their imported worship.

RELIGIOUS TRADITIONS AND OFFICIAL WORSHIP

Except for its baroque churches, which are a pale shadow of the magnificent temples scattered throughout the length and breadth of Asia, Filipino religious culture has no stone monument to sing its praises. The geographical location of the Philippine islands isolated their inhabitants from the cultural and religious exchanges among ancient Asian civilizations. They knew neither the wisdom of Confucius nor the mystic ways of Hinduism. The Filipino religious culture we know today began with the coming of Spanish missionaries. Unlike those of the rest of Asia, it is neither heavy with age nor buttressed on the bedrock of Asian religions. Rather, it is a synthesis of Western religiosity and of the native cultural expression of Filipinos.

Filipino culture is inconceivable without its popular religious rituals. These are town celebrations held outside the church building, often without ecclesiastical ministry. They range from the simplest family rituals to the most elaborate town processions, religious dances and theatrical religious presentations. These the people perform with a characteristic flair for drama and colourful festivity, abandon and spontaneity. It is here that they are able to let loose their pent-up zest for external celebrations which the sombreness of the official liturgy restrains. That is why, during the Easter Triduum, when most of the folk 'liturgies' are held side by side the official liturgy, there is an atmosphere of festivity, of community celebration and activity, in short, of a town *fiesta*.

The Spanish missionaries who introduced European religious traditions of the period or Christianized existing religious rituals were instrumental to the development of Filipino religious culture. Historians trace the festival of *Ati-atihan* to the yearly descent of the native Ati to the plains of Panay island to receive food in exchange for a dance demonstration. Today it is a costume festival of street dancing and merrymaking in honor of the child Jesus. Historians also see Christianized rituals in *Flores de Mayo* (daily offering of flowers to the Blessed Virgin in the month of May), fluvial processions in honour of the patron saints of riverside towns, and religious fertility dances before the images of saints. The other popular religious traditions are of European origin and are closely tied to liturgical celebrations. Examples of these are 'liturgical plays' which flourished in Europe from the fourteenth century until the age of the baroque. Originally they were performed in church and they employed texts which were basically those of the Mass and the Divine Office. But when indecorous and comic elements crept in, many such plays were evicted from the church to the town square. This explains why in the Philippines no 'liturgical plays' have traditionally been held inside the church, in spite of their affinity with the official worship. For they are in fact popular reenactments (often flavored with apocryphal ingredients) of the events commemorated by the liturgical feasts. These plays follow the liturgical calendar closely, except when the Bureau of Tourism sponsors the Maytime *Santakrusan* during the Christmas holiday as an added treat for foreign tourists.

A brief description of some of the principal forms of Filipino folk 'liturgy' will illustrate its socio-religious value and its lasting impact on Filipino culture. On Christmas eve many towns observe the *Panuluyan*, which dramatizes the holy couple's search for shelter. Hours before midnight the statues of the blessed Virgin and Saint Joseph are brought in front of houses where the scene is re-enacted. In sung verses the chorus begs for hospitality but is rudely dismissed by the householders. This dramatic re-enactment is intended to leave a deep impression on Filipinos for whom hospitality is a highly prized virtue.

In Lent the *Pasion* is sung in various homes for an entire day or for several hours every day. Friends and neighbours drop in, sing a portion of the *Pasion* before the altar, and sit afterwards for a meal which retains a vague sacral overtone. The text, written in the seven major Filipino languages and consisting of some 3,150 rhymed stanzas of five lines each, is a narration of the history of salvation. It tells the story of creation and the fall, explains the mystery of the Trinity, touches on the incarnation, childhood and public ministry of Christ, and dwells at length on his passion, death, resurrection and ascension. The text concludes with Pentecost and the assumption of the Blessed Virgin, and reminds the readers of the last judgment, the reward of heaven and the punishment of hell. In spite of the work of ecclesiastical censorship in 1884, the text is not totally purged of its apocryphal elements. Nevertheless, the book is extremely didactic and, for many generations, was the only book of Christian catechesis available to the majority of Filipinos.

But the more dramatic folk 'liturgies' are those celebrated during Holy Week. On Palm Sunday the *Hosanna* is performed by children who sing the *Benedictus qui venit* and strew flower petals during the procession. At night the *Cenaculo* or passion play is staged. It begins with the story of the fall and concludes with the ascension. The play can run for several nights. But the drama reaches its climax on Good Friday morning, when the carrying of the cross is re-enacted along the main streets of the town by costumed performers. Jews and Roman soldiers recite (or extemporize on) verses of insult and condemnation and whip the *Cristo*, who is thrust down by the weight of the wooden cross. Pious women come out to feed him and offer food to the rest of the performers. In the evening a solemn procession with the images of the entombed Christ, the sorrowful Mother and a cortège of saints clad in mourning, accompanied by a band playing funeral marches, is held along the main streets. The final drama takes place at Easter dawn before the first Mass of the day. It is known as *Salubong* or *Santo Encuentro,* the meeting of Christ and his Mother on Easter morning. Two separate processions, one with the image of the risen Christ, the other with the image of the Blessed Virgin veiled in black, meet at the town square. A little girl, dressed like an angel, is lowered from the roof of the platform and slowly lifts the black veil, as she sings the *Regina coeli*. Then the two images are made to bow to each other three times as a sign of greeting. White doves are released, and a young girl, holding an ornamented banner, performs a ritual dance expressing Easter joy.

From these examples one can assess the value folk 'liturgies' have in the life of Filipinos. They enjoy popularity, because they are fully incarnated in the religious culture of the people. They foster community life, because they are an endeavor which demands community involvement and which nourishes interpersonal relationships. They continue to be held with increasing interest, because they are regarded by the people as genuine expressions of their cultural identity. On the level of religious experience, these folk traditions, more than official liturgy, have sustained the faith and religious fervour of Filipinos over four centuries. Having entered into the mainstream of popular religiosity, they have become institutionalized and permanent forms of catechetical instruction, suited to the baroque temperament of the people and easily accessible to all. Allowing for a negative aspect— they did not deepen the understanding of the liturgy itself, but detracted from it—one must admit that they are an indispensable ingredient of the religious culture of the nation.

But one cannot dwell on this subject without posing some questions on the relationship between folk 'liturgies' and the reformed Roman liturgy. Do the former harmonize with the spirit of the latter? Should they be left as they are, or incorporated in some fashion into the official worship of the Church? On March 16, 1971 the Congregation for Divine Worship allowed the *Salubong* to take the place of the entrance rite for the first Mass of Easter Sunday. This encouraged many to toy with the idea of integrating the *Panuluyan* into the Christmas liturgy. Integration is a welcome affirmation of the value attached by the Church to popular traditions and of their possible rôle in the formation of indigenous worship. But the question is more intricate and has more loose ends than one may suspect. For historically, at least in the Philippines, folk 'liturgies' were never intended to be part of official worship. Being popular celebrations, they will necessarily be characterized by spontaneity and improvisation. One can also ask whether their presence in the foreign world of the Roman liturgy will render this less foreign. Is integration of this kind enough to satisfy the demand to incarnate the official liturgy in the culture of the people?

TOWARDS AN INDIGENOUS FORM OF WORSHIP

The question of being a Filipino and a Christian boils down to the question of culture, and must consequently be viewed in the context of the nation's search for cultural identity. This is a movement which seeks to rediscover and foster traditional values and rituals which have shaped the Filipino character for many generations. Through the arts, mass media and nationalistic slogans, a sense of cultural pride has been re-awakened among a people who in the recent past discredited their own cultural heritage and embraced Western ways and values. For the Church this changed climate is a clear indication that the time for indigenization has come. As the prolongation in time and space of the incarnation of the Word of God, the Church must tend towards an incarnation of herself, in such a way that she can be regarded not only as the Church that dwells among the people of the Philippines, but also as the Filipino Church. After the example of Christ who became a Jew, the Church must become Filipino.

In this new venture two areas are given priority: Filipino theology and Filipino liturgy. Various attempts, mostly on individual initiative, have been made during the last fifteen years. Thanks to these efforts the foundation was laid for future work. In 1974 the question surfaced officially, when the Catholic hierarchy issued a pastoral letter on Mary which invoked the role of native values and traditions in Marian devotions. The following year the Bishops' Conference devoted its July session to a discussion of Filipino values and religiosity. And in January 1976 it accepted in principle the *Misa ng Bayang Pilipino,* a study on the indigenization of the Roman Mass, prepared by the Benedictines in association with Maryhill School of Theology.

Misa ng Bayang Pilipino (Mass of the Filipino People) is an attempt to translate the demand of incarnating the Church's worship in Filipino culture and to allow this to be transparent to the worshipping community. It views the Filipino as a person who treasures his own traditions. For this reason its text employs traditional forms of expression which stem from his thought and language pattern, while its ritual incorporates elements inspired by his religious culture. Without departing from the basic outline of the Roman Mass, the *Misa* has borrowed from Oriental liturgies those forms that better suit the Filipino temperament. Without prejudice to the Christian message proclaimed and celebrated by the liturgy, it aims to offer Filipinos a form of worship which they can easily identify as their own.

In the area of ritual, the *Misa* incorporates elements derived from Filipino cultural traditions. Flower petals, for example, are strewn on the aisle at the entrance rite, in order to create an atmosphere of festivity and to honour the cross carried by the priest. In keeping with the Filipino's exuberant but deeply religious character, the entrance rite, the veneration of Sacred Scripture, the eucharistic prayer and the blessing have been worked out to produce a dramatic effect, while they convey a religious dimension. For this reason, the cross and Sacred Scripture are raised aloft while the people sing a doxology, candles are ritually lit at the start of the eucharistic prayer as sign of solemn prayer, church bells are festively rung, and the people are blessed with the cross. The communion of the priest after the people evokes the Filipino custom that the host eats after the guest. It is a common practice among rich and poor families alike, and is one of the traditional social graces expressing hospitality. Finally, the sign of unity is placed at the rite of dismissal, as an act of bidding farewell which has a significant place in the social life of Filipinos. It is a moment of expressing reassurances of fellowship and unity.

But the *Misa*'s unique quality is found in its text which was formulated with a view not only to transmitting faithfully the liturgical content, but also to reflecting the thought and language pattern of the people. Although the ritual can create an indigenous atmosphere, it is not the main criterion for judging the depth of indigenization. That is why a painstaking effort was made to employ Filipino forms of expression which could convey the Christian mystery celebrated by the liturgy. Proverbs, maxims, aphorisms and the colourful idioms that defy translation were paraphrased and instilled with liturgical character. Through them Filipino values and religious sensitivity were made to permeate the prayer formulas. The text of the eucharistic prayer suggests values that the people have traditionally cherished, like gratitude and reciprocity, and exalts God's initiative and concern for man. The other texts, especially those of the offertory and communion, abound in paraphrases of Filipino maxims and proverbs on divine providence and on human endeavor and generosity.

CONCLUSION

The historical approach to liturgical renewal has brought to light the essential message of Christian worship. In spirit and form the liturgy of Vatican II resembles more closely its archetype. But this is only a preliminary step towards a living liturgy. There remains the task of translating the message into the culture and religious traditions of the people. While there is a danger that cultural 'encumbrances' obscure the transparency of the liturgy, there is equally a danger that the liturgy will be reduced to a historical monument with no relevance to the daily experience of the worshipping community.

The adaptation of the liturgy to culture and religious traditions is thus an imperative.

Bibliography

D. Amalorpavadass, *Towards Indigenization of the Liturgy* (Bangalore, 1971).

E. Bazaco, *Culture of the Early Filipinos* (Manila, 1936).

M. Bernad, 'Philippine Culture and Filipino Identity', in *Philippine Studies* 19 (1971), pp. 573–92.

B. Botte, 'Le probelème de l'adaptation en liturgie', in *Revue du Clergé Africain* (June 1963), 307–30.

J. Bulatao, 'Changing Social Values', in *Philippine Studies* 10 (1962), pp. 206–14.

J. Carroll, 'The Filipino Dilemma', in *Solidarity* (Nov. 1968), pp. 60–68.

H. De La Costa, *Asia and the Philippines* (Manila, 1967).

V. Gorospe, 'Christian Renewal and Filipino Values', in *Philippine Studies* 14 (1966), pp. 191–227.

P. Gowing and W. H. Scott (eds.), *Acculturation in the Philippines* (Quezon City, 1971).

A. Manuud (ed.), *Brown Heritage, Essays on Philippine Cultural Tradition and Literature* (Quezon City, 1967).

L. Mercado, 'Filipino Thought', in *Philippine Studies* 20 (1972), pp. 207–72.

Y. Raguin, 'Indigenization of the Church', in *Teaching All Nations* 6 (1969), pp. 151–68.

J. Rich, 'Religious Acculturation in the Philippines', in *Practical Anthropology* 17 (1970), pp. 196–209.

R. Stauffer, 'The Need to Domesticate Foreign Models', in *Solidarity* (Apr. 1972), pp. 53–63.

Klemens Richter

Rites and Symbols in an Industrial Culture as Illustrated by Their Use in a Socialist Context

THE QUEST FOR MEANINGFUL SYMBOLS

LITURGIOLOGY needs to take far more serious notice of meaningful symbols in an industrial culture if we want to find out whether symbol and rite still have a valuable rôle to play in our society and what kind of symbols can still be understood today. The quest for the kind of gesture or token which may introduce our modern life and social structures into liturgical usage has hardly begun. It is no doubt true 'that banners are still raised and lowered, hair is still worn ostentatiously long or short, flowers are still given for a birthday, medals and cups are still distributed and accepted, parades are still held and the salute taken, and candles are still bought and lit'.[1] But we still have to leave it to the research undertaken by sociology, social psychology, the various communications sciences and particularly semiotics, which liturgiologists have so far hardly taken any notice of,[2] to make the necessary information available. Yet there have been some remarkable studies. There is, for instance, Robert Bellah's work on what he calls America's bourgeois religion, and his comparative study of the inaugural addresses of all America's presidents, simply to trace the development of a coherent non-ecclesiastical religion in the history of the U.S.A.[3] Then Thomas Luckmann has spelled out the fact that in modern industrial society religion has no longer the monopoly of social-religious institutions and the consequent challenge to the theologians.[4] Values and interpretations are conveyed by the most varied agents of socialization. In a sense there is a wide enough choice which leaves everyone free to follow his own bent. Peter Berger demands of theologians that they should look for the 'signs of transcendence' which may be discovered in modern secularized industrial society.[5] Access to this can only be found in that timeless experience of man which is beyond any measurable empirical basis. Berger mentions games, hope, our need for order, and our sense of what is evil and what is comical. Josef Pieper and Harvey Cox have reminded us that man's need to celebrate must be seen as one of the ways in which he approaches the transcendental.[6]

The complexity of symbols as a category cannot be contained by the traditional limits of a scientific discipline. Psychologists analyze the meaning of symbols for a person by bringing in methods of projection, anthropologists examine the function of symbols in their respective cultures, and architects are concerned with the symbolic implications of a given locality. There is as yet no uniform method of symbolic analysis. Most studies in this field admit that the transmission of values—the content of a philosophy of life or a faith—cannot be described as a simple sociological process. Every social group demands a socialization process which ensures the transmission of its specific socio-cultural heritage. Here symbols have a decisive role to play.[7] This socialization process embraces the appropriate value systems, norms, symbols and the general value-oriented behaviour patterns which those in charge of this process in the specific association pass on to the individual member who then learns and assimilates it.[8] In the context of the institutionalization which will take place and is indispensable for the continuity of these values and norms, certain actions will develop into a ritual with a symbolic character. As the means of communication the symbol, whether a word, a gesture or an action, will then be the basis for the individual member's experience of a value within the group.[9] That such symbolic actions can even today be immediately experienced in an almost religious sense has been pointed out by Heinrich Böll: 'There is the "sanctity" of a few puffs of a cigarette which a man experiences in himself but which, because he got it from the mouth of an imprisoned German captain, becomes a hymn and a litany since smoking means here more than tobacco for a chain-smoker: it has become the expression of brotherhood, compassion, a common embodiment of love . . . There are other situations with a similar kind of sacramentality about them, such as, perhaps, the sharing of bread and water in the prison of Brest, which took place under the eyes and leadership of Kopelev: he became a priest, almost a high priest, of bread and water. Whether in a camp or cell, one remembered the significance of this sharer of bread, a significance filled with absolute, almost sacred trust (anyone violating this trust really committed sacrilege)'.[10]

A rite can be understood as man's response to situations where there is otherwise simply no effective way of dealing with them.[11] The ritual tempers the feeling of uncertainty. Instead of uncontrolled outbursts when, for instance, faced with somebody's death, there are certain socially ordained things to be done. When the individual or the community can find no such meaningful outlet in such a social ritual a person's balance may often become pathologically disturbed or he may try to make up his own individual and neurotic substitute for collectively available standardized rites.[12] Every social grouping needs typical arrangements, ways of communicating through actions, through which it can discover and express its own image. A party without organized party meetings is unthinkable. The point here is the genuine coming-together which leads to the constitution of the party. And this holds everywhere, whether for a family celebration or the General Assembly of the United Nations. On such occasions these basic and typical organized events bring out the real matter which is the main concern of the particular group. This matter determines the shape of events and draws the participants together in a definite social relationship with each other. These structures through which a group is actively constituted and communicates are closely linked with the ways in which it pursues its purpose from day to day. The symbolism of vast party conferences is futile if not followed up by a daily slogging at publicity, increasing membership, and so on. On the other hand, all this daily labour will lose its sense of direction if there are no representative structures and events.

In all this, however, there is a particular problem which bristles with needs for socially recognized measures. It is the problem of passing from one phase of life to another; for example, from the unmarried state to marriage, from health to sickness, from innocence to guilt, and so on. The rites corresponding to these transition-states have for a long time been called 'rites of passage'.[13] Whereas rites are on the one hand actions which provide a response to what is out of the ordinary, they are also themselves a breakthrough of the daily routine. This holds for rites which are meant to produce conditions of ectasy and trance. Such kinds of achieving a socially standardized condition of being 'beside oneself' liberate a person from the rules and regulations that determine normal behaviour. In the Christian West the carnival may well be such a ritual suspension of ordinary everyday life. In view of the over-abundance of thrills and attractions, particularly in an industrial society, man is simply bound 'to reduce the endless number of anthropologically possible ways of behaviour to a limited number

of activities which comply with social norms, are approved and consequently foreseeable and calculable'.[14] This is the only way of ensuring
some security and stability. And only in so far as the industrial society
can develop these kind of rites, will it be able to cope without anxiety.
How rarely this is in fact the case today can easily be seen in the steep
rise in cases of neurotic illness.

Whether we look at it before or after the present state of affairs,
we have to hold on to the fact that western industrial societies provide
no or only very feeble secularized rites for the decisive phases of man's
life. Birth, marriage, guilt, illness and death are, in so far as their ritual
expression is concerned, today as in the past practically the exclusive
prerogative of the Churches which, in this ritual field, have a
monopoly. In so far as marriages and funerals are concerned, there
are in the United States at least some competing social institutions
whose commercial success proves only too convincingly how deep
man's need is for some rite which expresses his behaviour symbolically.
At the same time these enterprises seem to show that, in principle, it is
easy to find substitutes for the Churches in this field. Where such
competing rite-merchants fail, the Churches are now, as in the past,
still purely functional. It is, however, possible that this demand for
ecclesiastical rites has less to do with the contents of the Christian faith
than with the fact that the Churches have a monopoly of ritual. Where
the interests of the State encourage people to leave the Church as, for
instance, in the German Democratic Republic, the main measure is an
attempt to break the Church's ritual monopoly. The State then creates
its own symbolic actions which are meant to provide the central crises
of man's life with a specific interpretation but also with a ritual
expression.

RITES AND RITUAL IN A SOCIALIST CONTEXT

While in our western world we find it difficult to understand rites as
'the embodiment of a fantasy' which may have 'a liberating effect'[15]
and is a necessity for any human community it seems less difficult
for society in the socialist states to fit the key-points of man's existence
into the social context by some form of celebration. Thus an internal
party report of the Socialist Unity Party of Germany (SED) from
Stalinstadt (today: Eisenhüttenstadt) mentioned already in February
1959: 'The labourers' class of the German Democratic Republic and its
leading party are, on the basis of their philosophy of dialectical
materialism and with the assistance of the power of the socialist State,
beginning to attach a ceremonial quality to birth, marriage and death
as events in the life of the growing socialist community'.[16] According

to these public reports[17] the party leadership in the GDR aims at replacing baptism, communion, confirmation, ecclesiastical wedding and funeral by atheistic events: 'It is no longer the faith and individually cultivated needs that have to be satisfied but rather the kinds of awareness and political requirements laid down by the communist State. The intimate domain of the individual has been degraded to a publicly managed affair and man's dignity has been radically revalued. Hence, the atheistic ceremonies and rites are justified as the expression of a new self-awareness'.[18]

With this western criticism of the socialist ritual there has been in recent years a growing criticism by Christians of their own worship. This comes out in all kinds of demands made concerning the religious ceremonies which accompany a Christian's life from the cradle to the grave: they should use a language which is understood today, teach more about how to live in a human community, be far less centrally organized and abandon fixed texts and rites in favour of more freedom in their formulation.[19] We should give up the idea that religion is a purely private affair and break through the kind of individualism that is still so widespread today in order to bring out the sense of communal responsibility. The official reform of the liturgy has failed to achieve this in any adequate measure. But this is precisely what the organizers of the socialist ritual celebrations mean to be the basic distinguishing mark of their way of celebrating birth, the initiation into the community, marriage and death.

There is no doubt that these socialist celebrations were also introduced in order to oust or at least replace the corresponding Christian ceremonies for those who are no longer able to go completely along with the faith of the Church. Thus we read in the main publication of the SED: 'The aftermath and prejudices of the past hamper the activity of the working population. This is why the building up of a communist, social awareness . . . requires propagation and introduction of new socialist traditions and customs which leave constantly less room for religious festivals, customs and rites'.[20] Even the Chairman of the Christian Democratic Union in the GDR, Gerald Götting, considers it normal that 'an articulate religionless world should develop its own ceremonies for special events in the individual's life. For a long time only the Church made this kind of thing available, but this period is now coming to an end. The new socialist ceremonies are not the answer to the breakdown of popular religion at the right moment, but the expression of a world without religion'.[21] These statements correspond altogether to the findings of modern sociology. If somebody has no or hardly any knowledge of the symbols, does not accept their inner meaning and makes no attempt whatever to comply with the behavioural demands which may flow from these symbols, he is by the same token recognized as a non-member. Social and particularly religious symbols are indispensable for the distinction between members and non-members in any secondary group. When the symbols disappear the wider group loses the distinctness of its image and gradually slips into disintegration'.[22] Every social group, however informal, will soon develop its own ritual which will shape its everyday life, or it will collapse. It can be taken as a fact that every community needs the communal activity of its members in order to create and maintain the sense of belonging together. Thus it makes sure of its common conviction, its common life-style and its common faith through specific rites for definite occasions, particularly also on the occasions of birth, marriage and death.

Here one should beware of too glibly asserting that socialist rites are only a way of fighting the Church by open or concealed means. This element may well play a part and even be given more or less emphasis by the political authorities. Yet the inherent value of these ceremonies and their function in the building up of the socialist community should not be underrated. It may well be that they are only considered as a motivating force in the fight with the Church where an individual is more or less directly forced to make use of this ceremonial. Up till the present this actually holds only for the party initiation rite of the young in the German Democratic Republic and the other States that belong to the socialist camp. The Churches have taken the line that the development of these socialist rites was a direct attack on their sphere of influence. But does this help them to understand their own sacraments? They are often accused, also among ourselves, that they want to drive as many people as possible to the sacraments, regardless of what these people really believe. If this is so it might well conceal the real reason which is that the Churches mean by their sphere of influence the continuation of the *status quo* and with it the situation of the 'popular Church' (*Volkskirche*). Could Götting then not be right when he wants the Church to offer its ecclesiastical ritual to its own Christians and not to busy itself with the solemnization of purely secular events like birth and marriage?

Both the Church and the Party celebrate the focal events of life with some solemnity. In these basic human situations a man experiences that he is inescapably involved in a material, biological and social world. But at the same time he looks for some meaning, some destiny, for the ultimate origin and future of his life. And so he wants to understand the meaning of his world. These basic situations can be interpreted in various ways: theistically, atheistically, fatalistically; or one can leave the question of meaning alone in the way of immanent humanism and sceptical agnosticism. Just as the Christian faith has always interpreted the various situations of man's life in its own way, so there is no reason why a community of people who hold a socialist and atheistic view of life should be barred from working out their own attitude to these situations by creating their own ways of celebrating them: 'The content of these festivities for the working population is provided by socialist humanism which is atheistic and recognizes no higher being than mankind itself as it works and struggles for freedom, democracy and socialism . . . These festivities become meaningful when this specific human endeavour will find itself in harmony with the general and universal'.[23] Since during the period of transition from capitalism to socialism one cannot assume that personal and communal interests will already coincide, it is the task of the State to use its socialist educational influence on parents, engaged couples or the bereaved, in the preparation for, and the conducting of, these festivities. For many years it was not clear how this should come about. The individual rites were immediately surrounded with a kind of arcane discipline. Only with the youth initiation was this different from the beginning. This was to be as far as possible compulsory for all fourteen-year-olds,[24] while the other rites would indeed be spread but were never seriously enforced for the larger sections of the population. Only for the last few years have these been regular agendas—somewhat like liturgical rituals—which contain instructions for the ceremonies, serve as textbooks and offer model addresses, songs and music, but also explanations of the meaning of the rites.[25] It looks almost as if the Party has for a long time tried to evade this kind of publication. From the point of view of the claim to be informative and Marxist these texts perhaps do not altogether fit into the concept of scientific socialism.

The individual rites have undergone a continuing development. Since the middle nineteen-fifties they have played their part in the German Democratic Republic. The somewhat aggressive claims that prevailed in the beginning are not in the more recent books—not a word about Church or Christianity. Even in public there is barely any propaganda on these lines. While at first these socialist festivities were highlighted in the press, this is rarely the case today: this may possibly mean that the response is relatively weak. The funeral ceremony, however, is an exception. Since, in view of increasing secularization—it is, for instance, estimated that in the GDR hardly twenty-five per cent of the children are still baptized[26]—birth and marriage can also be celebrated within the family circle, this is more difficult in the case of a funeral. Here socialist funeral orators are also called upon by citizens who are otherwise not terribly interested in a proper 'socialist burial'. It is

remarkable that in many towns these funeral orators already undertake a kind of pastoral function and often are the confidants of older
people. Here only those persons are asked for 'who are exemplary
from the politico-moral point of view and capable of doing what is
asked of them: that is, that they are real orators'.[27] These people are
increasingly younger people who have finished their philosophy course
at a university.

At the 'name dedication' (*Namensweihe*), which is distinct from the
giving of the name and birth registration and takes place about twelve
to eighteen months after birth, several children are usually brought
into the actual celebration. This lasts about thirty minutes and contains
the following parts. Guests and godparents take their places. As some
music is being played the parents and children come into the room,
accompanied by an official speaker and officials of the business or
factory. After a recitation there follow the official speech and the
signing of the documents by parents and godparents and also the
solemn commitment. This 'name dedication' is clearly related to the
community: the promise of future happiness by the community as a
wish expressed for life at present. The following features may be
mentioned here: the presentation of a glass of wine, the decoration of
the room, festive music, the good wishes of those present in the context
of the occasion. The parents and godparents bind themselves to guide
the child's life towards socialism: 'We, the parents and godparents,
will do everything to bring up the child in the spirit of peace, friend-
ship between the nations and love for our State, and to ensure a happy
future for him in socialism'. This pledge is meant to give the citizens an
emotional bond with the State and its philosophy: the individual
promises loyalty to the community, and in return the community
will protect him and encourage him in his commitment to socialism.

Every socialist wedding is assumed to be preceded by a preparatory
talk which also explains the basic principles which underlie the celebration. Here the directives state: 'The method of these talks must be
based on the firm and patient persuasion of Marxist-Leninism. This
method contains a provocative initiative on the part of the speaker and
a guarantee of the freedom to decide on the part of his interlocutor'.
The celebration itself is in two parts and consists of the marriage
pledge and the civil wedding. The greeting is followed in the form of
questions and answers, the actual contracting of the marriage, the
entry into the marriage register, the exchange of rings, the address
and the socialist pledge. This binds the partners to pursue the aims of
the workers' and farmers' State: 'Responsible for one another and
ourselves, we solemnly promise all productive people . . . to build our
marriage, here and now established in mutual love as a partnership for

the whole of life. We promise all those that work to increase what has been achieved by socialism and the political power of workers and farmers with the strength of common action. We promise one another attentive respect, care and help in need, mutual assistance towards professional and cultural development, to decide things together, and indissoluble fidelity'.

Youth initiation is also part of the socialist rites. This also proceeds through word and sign—the reading of passages from the documents that teach the Marxist way to salvation, festive dress, music and singing, room decoration, banners, and so on. The preparation for this ceremony—an initiation rite for incorporation into the working world of socialism—has a materialistic and atheistic character. Yet the ceremony and its solemn pledge are not an explicit confession of atheism. Practically all young people are urged to pass through this rite. It has the kind of features that are well known in the domain of the Church through mass-confirmation or first communion, from the social compulsion to drink among the well-to-do to alcoholism, from conforming to the attitude of the majority to the private indifference of those who merely endure the festivity.

There is therefore no question that symbolic activities are very important today for socialization, nor that ritually supported ways of behaviour have far more influence on socialization within a given group than the verbalisation of educational principles. Here it is always important that these ritually supported activities are not given the lie by the way in which those who carry out and transmit them lead the rest of their own lives.[28] Symbolic activities are only credible where they correspond to the whole of life. The decisive question, however, is what kind of ritual symbolic activity suits people who live in an industrial and technological society. To this must be added that in the past rites could develop over long periods of time which were then recognized as viable and taken over by wider areas. 'Here the problem arises whether our whole social communication system in which we live does not hamper the development of rites, symbols and celebrations . . . by the fact that what is happening in one or other region under special conditions is then already observed on a universal scale and either uncritically taken over or too hastily condemned as wild growth'.[29] The problem of our society as compared with the past lies in that rational planning which makes it now hardly possible to get familiarized with ritual events. 'Rational planning is time-intensive while the getting familiarized with rites which is precisely the surest way towards reconciliation is, on the contrary time-demanding. The ritualised agreements of a community only make life worth living in the experience of the members of the group. The development of these circumscribed laws takes, however, place on a different level from that of planning awareness, namely in events that have their roots in the unconscious.

Looking back at history we see that ways of ritualized behaviour are, once established, essentially more stable than has been the case with the majority of codified rules and regulations'.[30]

The Church, however, will find it difficult to find its bearings with regard to the symbols and their meaning of an industrial culture whatever their individual appearance. Christian communities are concerned with specific spiritual experiences. 'This should then be the area where new ways of expressing the faith can be discovered and grow, but where at the same time old ways or forms could be found again and newly understood. Neither the simple repetition of doctrinaire statements nor the rational planning of new rites . . . will provide the solution, but only the way towards a growing sense of faith. And it will be along this way that new ways of ritual behaviour can be found and tested in the life of the Church'.[31]

Translated by Theo Weston

Notes

1. H. Hucke and H. Rennings, *Die gottesdienstlichen Versammlungen der Gemeinde* (Pastorale 2) (Mainz, 1973), p. 38.
2. Cf. U. Eco, *La struttura Assente* (Milan, 1968).
3. R. Bellah, 'Civil Religion in America', in *Daedalus* 96 (1967), 1, pp. 1–22.
4. T. Luckmann, *The Invisible Religion* (New York, 1967).
5. P. Berger, *A Rumour of Angels* (New York, 1969).
6. J. Pieper, *Musze und Kult* (Munich, 7th ed., 1965); H. Cox, *The Feast of Fools* (Cambridge, Mass., 1969).
7. Cf. L. A. Vaskovics, 'Religionssoziologische Aspekte der Sozialisation wertorientierter Verhaltnisformen', in *Internationales Jahrbuch für Religionssoziologie* 3 (1967), pp. 115–46.
8. *Ibid.*, p. 121.
9. *Ibid.*, p. 121.
10. H. Böll, 'Nachwort', in L. Kopelew, *Aufbewahren für alle Zeit* (Hamburg, 1976), p. 604; original ed.: *Chranit' večno* (1975).
11. B. Malinowski, *Magic, Science and Religion* (Glencoe, 1948).
12. A. Hahn, *Religion und der Verlust der Sinngebung* (Frankfurt/New York, 1974), pp. 71ff.
13. A. V. Gennep, *Les Rites de Passage* (Paris, 1908).
14. A. Hahn, *op. cit.*, p. 75.
15. H. Cox, *op. cit.*
16. *Grundsätze und Erfahrungen bei der Gestaltung sozialistischer Feierlichkeiten* (February 1959), Az.: Kd 2431/58 III K (mimeogr.).

17. Cf. W. Maser, *Der Kampf der SED gegen die Kirche (Freiheit und Ordnung* 24) (Mannheim, 1962); *idem, Genossen beten nicht* (Cologne, 1963); F. G. Hermann, *Der Kampf gegen Religion und Kirche in der Sowjetischen Besatzungszone Deutschlands* (Stuttgart, 1966).

18. Cf. Maser, *Der Kampf,* p. 17.

19. See E. J. Lengeling, 'Liturgie im Wandel der Gesellschaft und der Kirche', in J. Schreiner (ed.), *Die Kirche im Wandel der Gesellschaft,* (Würzburg, 1970), p. 196.

20. I. R. Rachimova, 'Der XXIV. Parteitag der KPdSU und einige Fragen der atheistischen Erziehung' in *Neues Deutschland,* 26 Feb. 1972 (E. Berlin).

21. Ms. of 1972. Gerald Götting is also President of the People's Chamber in the Parliament of the German Democratic Republic.

22. H. J. Helle, 'Symbol und Gottesdienst', in H. G. Schmidt (ed.), *Zum Gottesdienst morgen* (Wuppertal/Munich, 1969), pp. 24–32.

23. Cf. note 16.

24. In 1976 about 97% = 280,000 of all fourteen-year-olds took part.

25. The texts are published by the Zentralhaus für Kulturarbeit in Leipzig: *Sei willkommen Kind. Empfehlungen für die Namensweihe,* 1973; *Offen steht das Tor des Lebens. Empfehlungen für die Jugendweihe,* 1973; *Hochzeit machen. Material für die Fest- und Feiergestaltung,* 1974; *Alles hat am Ende sich gelohnt. Material für weltliche Trauerfeiern,* 1973.

26. The estimates are based on data provided by parish priests. No official statistics have been researched by the State.

27. See note 26.

28. A. Mitscherlich, 'Pubertät und Tradition' in L. V. Friedeburg (ed.), *Jugend in der modernen Gesellschaft* (Cologne, 4th ed., 1967), pp. 299f.

29. L. Bertsch, 'Die "Ritualisten" als Frage an die Riten und Symbole der Kirche', in K. Forster (ed.), *Zur Zukunft von Glaube und Kirche* (Freiburg, 1973), p. 92.

30. Cf. Mitscherlich, *op. cit.,* pp. 290f.

31. Cf. Bertsch, *op. cit.,* pp. 96f.

Joan Llopis

Popular Religion in Spain: The Nature of Current Theological Discussion

POPULAR religion has only recently claimed its share of theological interest in Spain. After the enthusiastic welcome for the novel theology of secularization,[1] another era is upon us now that this topic warrants the new and considered opinion of theologians, pastoral experts and liturgists.

As Fernando Urbina has pointed out,[2] since the late nineteen-sixties the subject of popular religion has been simultaneously broached from several quarters and from widely different angles. First, a return to popular sources is being urged by Latin American theologians and pastoral experts; in the second place, Europe has undertaken a critical review of its own pastoral assumptions in the matter; thirdly, sacral and religious values are being rediscovered by contemporary spiritual movements. All of this has been felt in pastoral and theological circles in Spain: articles have appeared in various journals and special groups have been set up to study and discuss the theme, which has even found its way to the agenda of some episcopal meetings.

The leading voice has probably been that of the Latin American theologians and pastoral experts. A seminar on 'Faith and Social Change in Latin America' held in Escorial in 1972 brought forth a spirited defence of popular religion. In 1974, the Ninth Colloquium organized in Avila by the magazine *Pastoral Misionera* was devoted exclusively to the subject, which was treated within a frame of reference very similar to the Latin Americans.

In a brief article, Segundo Galilea[3] mentions how Latin American pastoral thought, influenced both by the ascendancy of popular culture and the theology of liberation, proceeded to turn the tables on the critics of folk piety: 'As greater value was set on the defence of popular culture, of which religion is an integral part, the theology of liberation and its pastoral pronouncements came round to the idea that the people's religious legacy was not necessarily conformist or alienating'.

On the other hand, the rehabilitation of popular religion can also be advanced by 'right-wing' elements who, in their desire to stop the forces that might deliver the masses from their age-old domination and subservience, would bind the people to religious practices engendered by an archaic social conscience. In this regard it is interesting to note that at the Avila Colloquium mentioned above, it was precisely the participants from Andalusia, whose pastoral work takes place in the truly popular milieu of villages and slums, who sounded the clearest warning about the dangers of an excessively enthusiastic or ingenuous approach to popular religion.

Theological speculation on this subject is, obviously, so far from development in Spain that it cannot be accounted for with any degree of accuracy. One can speak of attempts, of overtures, of preliminary probes; that is what I shall do in this paper, fully aware of the makeshift nature of their results. Although every author I present has a theological interest in the theme, each favours a different approach. Based on these differences I shall try to give a rudimentary classification of their work.

THE PHENOMENOLOGICAL APPROACH

Juan de Dios Martín Velasco is the scholar most concerned with the phenomenological aspect of the theme, or with the definition of its terms.[4] In the article in reference, he attempts to describe the nature of popular religion as exactly as possible but without losing sight of the dynamic development to which it is constantly subject.

He points to three possible meanings of the adjective 'popular' as applied to religion. The first is synonymous with 'working class'; in this sense, 'popular Christianity' would denote a Church committed to the people, sharing in their destiny, and joining in their struggle for liberation. Those who favour this definition hold piety in such contempt, however, that, in this context, the expression is virtually null and void. In the second instance it means traditional or folkloric. Finally, it is used to describe all things that bear upon the average man—the man in the street who has not had any special type of education or assumed any special responsibilities.

In his analysis, Martín Velasco limits himself to the last two meanings of the word.

He begins by defining popular religion as the complex of religious expressions or mediations emerging in and from the people and which, going from mouth to mouth, are handed down traditionally. Its traits bring it in line with those religions which some sources have defined as cosmico-biological, that is, creeds in which the sacred is closely related to Nature and its cycles, and in which human life constitutes an integral part of the life of the cosmos. Since their grasp of the sacred is so closely related to natural phenomena, these religions set little store by human history and the freedom and enterprise which promote it.

It would seem that traditional religion is rapidly becoming extinct. But we must also admit that the massive, impersonal culture of modern times is beginning to show signs of wear and tear and that, under cover of more or less 'wild' procedures, there are hints of a renaissance aimed at bringing popular religion back to its traditional mainstream.

Next, Martín Velasco analyzes what he calls 'popularized religion'. This is the religion of the average man, of the rank and file of the faithful, as opposed to that professed by the educated or militant believer or the leading member of a religious organization. It has several distinctive traits: it is practical; the sacral pervades it to a considerable extent; it is of a devotional nature, and has an enormous need of assurances. Based more on habit than tradition, it has all the earmarks of a routine endeavour. Of its decline there can be no doubt; one of its surest proofs is the diminishing index of so-called religious observance. And yet new variations of this type of religion keep turning up, promoted by spiritual or pastoral movements which find their inspiration at various levels of the official religious establishment.

Martín Velasco disregards this popularized observance, believing it to be a departure from the truly popular norm brought about by the urge to 'officialize' all worship. In contrast he upholds the value of genuinely popular religion. As he himself declares:

The assessment of popular religion must begin by making clear the difference between piety and religion, and between piety and faith. This difference has been blithely invoked by some theologians and pastoral experts as the final proof against piety. A more dispassionate test would lead us to the conclusion that neither religion nor faith, are, in effect, synonymous with piety. But at the same time we must admit that there can be no religion, and no faith, if piety is lacking. As a corporeal, articulate being whose life is inevitably bound up with objects, man can enter into partnership with the Mystery only if he resorts to those depths and powers in his own makeup whose function it is to mediate between him and this non-objective Reality, bringing forth piety in all its manifestations. These manifestations are not to be identified with the God to whom they point; but without them man cannot enter into a human relationship with him.

THE SOCIO-HISTORICAL APPROACH

Under this heading I shall not refer to the strictly sociological or historical aspects of the theme—already mentioned in the first part of this paper—but to theological studies based on research undertaken by sociologists and historians.

The most stimulating author in this field is Aurelio L. Orensanz.[5] The first of the works I cite—a short but substantial book—is an objective account of the religious aspect of the post-Civil War period in Spain, 'one of the least examined but most urgently in need of study'. It covers the twenty-five years between 1940 and 1965, divided into three periods: the forties, the fifties, and sixties. The first, defined as the era of *total piety*, had all the flavour of a mission to the masses set up in accordance with pastoral directives. Religion, understood solely in terms of such a mission and of the complex pastoral work it entails, pervaded every facet of contemporary life. Next came the period of *personal piety*, with the Cursillo movement as its norm. Before analyzing it, Orensanz points to three unique developments in the Spain of the fifties: the critical assessment of Spanish piety undertaken by the nation's own intellectuals (Aranguren in particular); the optimistic, mass-oriented renewal promoted by the publications of the *Propaganda Popular Católica*; and the emergence of new directions in sacred art, with emphasis on authenticity of expression and simplicity in the choice of materials and forms. These developments were as many cracks in the solid picture of the post-Civil War Church, and the agents of a transition to a personal brand of piety. The third period, a time of new awareness, was the period of *the Gospel and reality*. Its model was the *Juventudes Obreras Católicas* (Young Catholic Workers) movement, which had great influence on the structural rationale of pastoral work and, more concretely, on the concept of the parish as a community.

In the second article listed under his name, Orensanz rounds off his comments on the past with a look at the future. What might be in the offing, in his opinion, is what he calls the 'Anglicanization' of Spanish Catholicism. Pointing to the fact that—unlike French or Italian Catholicism or the Protestantism of Central Europe—Anglicanism has lived through the most intense periods of industrialization, urbanization and democratization without losing its national eminence on the religious plane, Orensanz suggests that a similar experience could be in store for the Church in Spain.

If so, it would mean several things: a continuation of the symbiosis between the Spanish temper and Catholicism, with the survival of the latter as a distinctive national feature; the persistence of a high index of 'routine' religious practices (baptism, first communion, and so on) accompanied by a drop in regular observance; in the wider social sphere, the total irrelevance of the hierarchy's views on morals, political options, and so on, as against a growing number of strident protests, demonstrations or gestures on the part of certain groups or bishops or members of the clergy; and in the areas of culture, labor relations and politics, the consolidation of a climate from which specifically Catholic values and interests are totally absent. In sum, it would mean a Catholicism with a disembodied, diluted political weight, useful only as window dressing on solemn or state occasions—a faith which has become a 'reserve fund', taken out of circulation and unrelated to the risks and achievements of the day. If such an 'Anglicanization' is to be avoided, Orensanz believes that pastoral work must be disengaged from the traditional parish structure without delay, and that there must be a contribution to, and witness in, the intellectual, literary and artistic worlds and the pledge of allegiance to a historical process whose sights are really fixed on tomorrow, not on yesterday or the day before.

Antonio Bernard[6] is another author whose work is based on sociological findings, and who attempts to uphold the genuinely Christian values inherent in many popular religious practices in Spain.

THE PASTORAL APPROACH

This leads us directly to those theologians interested mainly in the pastoral aspects of the question. One of them, already referred to, is Fernando Urbina.[7] He believes there is an urgent need to consider the dialectical possibilities inherent in the two spheres of the pastoral ministry: with groups noted for their committed and militant faith, it might be possible to compensate for their lack of religious, mystic and sacramental sensibility through a synthesis of faith and piety, the prophetic and the liturgical, action and contemplation; when working among those sectors of the population steeped in what is known as popular religion, it might be possible to prepare them for an adult faith through an education that builds on the religious convictions they already possess.

Another valuable contribution—this one dealing concretely with the liturgical aspects of the theme—has been made by Dionisio Borobio,[8] who sets forth a number of suggestions based on Vatican II's Constitution on the Liturgy and Paul VI's apostolic exhortation, *Marialis Cultus*. Borobio draws up a list of criteria to be used in assessing the diverse manifestations of popular religion—not in order to 'bring the dead back to life' but rather in an effort to approach the sensibility of the people from within.

His main points for judging the soundness of popular religion are the following:

Its contents must be objectively credible and charged with meaning. If they are sustained by magic or taboos, if their underlying concepts are disingenuous or their fundamental references distorted, then we shall have come up against a twisted or debased brand of piety. Conversely, if the people are to find such contents credible and charged with meaning, they must reflect their own religious sensibilities.

If popular religion is genuine it must stem from life and tend to life. If it means an evasion or an escape from life's tragedies and hopes, or if there is a gulf between its expressions and vital experience, then it is a sham. On the other hand, popular religion is not to be identified with any ideology or school of thought, nor with political action or praxis. Above and beyond these elements, which it may contain, it remains primarily concerned with sensations, symbols, spontaneity, exuberance: its essence is the religious *fiesta*.

The re-examining and implementing of popular religion must itself be based on four criteria: (*a*) the biblical, which demands that priority be accorded the Word of God, that rituals and prayers be grounded in Scripture, that there be over-all harmony with the great messages of Christianity; (*b*) the liturgical, which means an orderly arrangement of devotions alongside sacramental and liturgical acts, in which they should culminate and of which they are a necessary extension; (*c*) the ecumenical, which presupposes an awareness of the problems and purposes of the ecumenical movement, eschewing sectarian attitudes and in communion with the other brethren; and (*d*) the anthropological, which requires a deep study of the social sciences so as to bring popular piety in line with their most solid and reliable findings.

According to Borobio, the true assessment of popular religion is a creative endeavour which 'cannot be carried out without the people but must be done with them and from the very heart of their lives. It is a creative task that must be widened, shared, handed back to the people so that they may feel bound up with it. This means an end to the monopoly of the clergy and an acceptance of the benefits and risks of spontaneity; it means that the people are no longer to be regarded as obedient children who must do as they're told, but as creative beings whose outpourings come from the depths of their belief'.

THE GLOBAL APPROACH

The contribution to the theology of popular religion made recently by Luis Maldonado has such wide scope that it deserves separate mention. At the Ninth Colloquium in Avila[9] Maldonado had already set forth the basic principles of his thought, which he had developed during the three academic years he spent directing a seminar on the subject at the School of Theology of the University of Salamanca, and which he has now brought forth in this most important book.[10]

Maldonado places his study in the framework of the new and ubiquitous concern for popular religion—a concern which is not a response to a trend pure and simple, but rather a reaction to certain crucial developments in contemporary life. Among these must be counted the change in political climate, with the people once again as the centre of activity; the cultural crisis of a techno-industrial society which is discovering its enormous drawbacks and searching for the new man in areas heretofore spurned by the rationalism of the Enlightenment—a rationalism which, having held sway from those days to our own, is itself showing signs of stress, and rather spectacular ones at that; and finally, the parallel shift of a theology which, after a period of inclination to the secular and political on the one hand and 'naked faith' on the other, is slowly realizing that it must widen its horizons once again in order to effect a synthesis of faith and religion, the sacred and the profane.

As an exponent of the theologians' change of direction, Maldonado quotes the principal architect of political theology, J. B. Metz, who in a lecture given in Madrid early in 1975 had this to say: 'What theology needs with the utmost urgency is the religious experience embodied in the people's symbols and tales . . . It must resort to them if it is not to starve . . . Now more than ever theology needs the religion, the mysticism and the religious experience of simple people as its bread'.

Maldonado's book is divided into three parts. The first consists of a classification and description of the main religious celebrations of the Spanish people. The second sets forth the main interpretative guidelines in popular religion and analyzes them in depth: the magic, the symbolic, the imaginary, the mystic, the festive, the farcical, the theatrical, the communal and the political. The third and last part of the book is a review of the links between popular religion and the liturgy across the centuries. The work ends on a semantic note with a searching look at the word 'people' in its diverse meanings.

A synthesis of the book is an impossible task in view of its essentially analytical nature. But this should not keep us from underlining its main concern, which is the discovery and understanding of the popular factor in the field of religion. In the author's sincere opinion theology, like secular culture, must return to the popular for inspiration. 'Far be it from us to turn the people into a myth or divinity', he says. 'That has been done often enough! One simply wishes to know them better, to meditate once again on certain values of theirs whose neglect or damage by bourgeois culture has been such, that they are on the point of disappearing'.

It is difficult to predict the course of theological speculation on this subject in Spain. What we are witnessing at this stage is an awakening of interest in the theme, certain preliminary analyses undertaken from a variety of angles and a few timid attempts to systematization. Whether or not this leads to an original, coherent school of thought will depend largely on the pastoral side of the work—which, for the moment, remains pretty much uncoordinated and even contradictory.

Translated by T. F. Buons

Notes

1. See bibliography in *Fe y nueva sensibilidad histórica* (Salamanca, 1972), pp. 395–467.

2. Fernando Urbina, 'Acercamiento al tema de la religiosidad popular', in *Phase* 15 (1975), pp. 335–44.

3. Segundo Galilea, 'Evangelización de la religiosidad popular. Dialéctica de nos "modelos" pastorales', in *Sal Terrae* 62 (1974), pp. 724–30.

4. Juan de Dios Martín Velasco, 'La fiesta. Estructura y morfología de una manifestación de la vida religiosa', in *Phase* 11 (1971), pp. 239–55; 'Religiosidad popular, cultura popular y evangelización', in *Equipos en misión* 18 (1974), pp. 17–34; 'Religiosidad popular, religiosidad popularizada y religión oficial', in *Pastoral misionera* 11 (1975), pp. 46–66.

5. Aurelio L. Orensanz, *Religiosidad popular española, 1940-1965* (Madrid, 1974); 'Religiosidad popular española, ¿crisis o extención?', in *Hechos y Dichos* 461 (1975), pp. 39–40.

6. Juan Antonio Bernard, 'Catolicismo tradicional-popular y acción pastoral en España', in *Sinite* 10 (1969), pp. 124–40; 'Sociología religiosa de las fiestas populares en el medio rural español: perspectivas pastorales', in *Phase* 10 (1970), pp. 283–96; *Pastoral de una fe madura. Diagnóstico sociorreligioso del catolicismo tradicional* (Madrid, 1972).

7. Besides the article cited in note 2, see Fernando Urbina, 'Opción misionera y religiosidad popular', in *Pastoral misionera* 11 (1975), pp. 3–13.

8. Dionisio Borogio, 'Religiosidad popular en la renovación litúrgica: criterios para una valoración', in *Phase* 15 (1975), pp. 345–64.

9. Luis Maldonado, 'Sugerencias preliminares para una valoración teológica de la religiosidad popular', in *Pastoral misionera* 11 (1975), pp. 67–83.

10. Luis Maldonado, *Religiosidad popular. Nostalgia de lo mágico* (Madrid, 1975).

Vicent Josep Sastre García

Popular Religion in Spain:
The Sociological Groundwork

IN the past few months popular religion has become a matter of some interest in Spain. The bishops of the South have made it the subject of an important document, several magazines have devoted special issues to the theme, and sociologists and pastoral experts have analyzed it in meetings and colloquia. In addition, two far from negligible in-depth studies have appeared in book form.[1]

Given the variety of approaches in the study of popular religion and its pastoral and theological corollaries, a definition of our own terms of reference is in order. By popular religion I mean, in the first place, all religious expressions which are natural to the masses as opposed to those favoured by minorities with a higher degree of culture and religious learning. I also class as 'popular' anything which springs from or survives in 'the people' at one or several removes from the institutional and the official. The present study is therefore contained within two parameters: first, the popular as opposed to the élitist, and, second, as distinct from the official-institutional.

Before turning to the contributions of sociological research in this field, let us cast a glance at the broad framework which the life of the national Church provides for popular religion in Spain, and at the factors which underlie current interest in this topic.

POPULAR RELIGION IN THE CONTEXT OF THE SPANISH CHURCH

The last decade in the life of the Spanish Church has been marked by a dynamic, Council-inspired renewal. As this renewal gained momentum, the institutional came nearer to the realities of Christian life, the hierarchy to the rest of God's people, and spiritually cultured minorities drew closer to the masses. So far however the masses and their religion have been the object, not the subject of this renewal. The mediocrity of its outcome is in fact the reason behind current interest in popular religion and its concrete expressions. Let us see how this state of affairs came about.

In the face of rapid social change and the emergence of a public conscience imbued with the Council's modern spirit, it had become obvious that the Church's official institutions were wide of the mark where the new Christian sensibilities were concerned. The reform of the liturgy came as the most 'visible' token of a rapprochement between the institutional and the new Christian climate. Sociological surveys proved the reform's massive appeal but they also revealed that the element of protagonism was lacking in its design. This absence of a popular element, and the creative participation it entails, has brought on a new 'conventionalism' from which escape is sought through domestic Eucharists or celebrations specially devised for small groups or for the young. Unfortunately most of these events lack popular flavour and time and again the participants will be drawn from the same culture and sophisticated minority. But let us drop the liturgical as a case in point and see how apostolic movements constitute yet another line of approach to the people and the realities of their lives.

Apostolic movements with a popular bent such as JOC and HOAC (*Juventudes Obreras Católicas, Hermandades Obreras de Acción Católica*) are traditional in Spain. They have turned their missionary and prophetic sights on the masses and obviously tried to become an integral part of working-class life and culture. Perhaps their spirit has leaned more towards the sapiential and triumphalistic than towards dialogue, hindering a full and fruitful interaction with popular religion. The search for the transcendental has engaged them less than the demands of justice, upsetting the balance between the latter and belief and polarizing their work on a political plane. This has helped to counter the notion of Christianity as an alienated creed but, as sociological research has proved, it has divorced the faith from its religious expressions.

Looking back over the past five years, however, perhaps the most extraordinary experience in the life of the Spanish Church has been the encounter between hierarchy and people. It began with bishops coming closer to priests—a trend which reached its climax with the Joint Assembly of 1971—and continued as priests drew nearer the masses. This common search for the renewal of the priesthood, its ministry and its commitment to the service of Christians has made such a lasting impression on the Spanish Church that the ghostly threat of democracy in ecclesiastical haunts has been powerless to dispel it. A comprehensive and exacting review of the situation at hand was followed by three years of reflection and study; in their wake came new attitudes and new interpretations of the ministry. The predominantly young and relatively abundant Spanish clergy found one more reason for approaching their people with an outlook less clerical, more in keeping with reality and in tune with the renewal posited by the Council. The keynotes of this encounter of the clergy's with the faithful have been many, ranging from a benevolent, accommodating paternalism to open clashes vis-à-vis popular and traditional religious expressions.

To put it briefly, the problem of the encounter with popular religion has been the problem of bringing the apex of a pyramid closer to its base, but without altering its pyramidal shape. As attitudes go, this one smacks of that old rule about 'governing for the people but without them'. Generally speaking it is the reason why religious expressions created by or ingrained in the people have been lost sight of, and why, on the other hand, the popular element has opposed certain drastic and sudden innovations which constitute an outrage to its religious sensibilities (witness slum churches totally denuded of images and other visual symbols charged with meaning in popular culture). Resistance to renewal has not been lacking, either, for reasons of attachment to tradition and routine.

NEW ATTITUDES TOWARDS POPULAR RELIGION

The belittling and undervaluation of popular religion seems to have touched bottom and at present the hierarchy, as sell as theologians and pastoral experts, are moving towards positions that are less extreme and more positive. It would seem that popular religion is not all magic, *fiesta* or folklore; nor does the magic, or the festive, appear now to be unrelated to the expression of faith. Several factors have been at work behind this change in values and attitudes.

The first is a growing awareness of the Church as the People of God, which has in turn suggested the image of a Church less conscious of its own summit and more attentive to the realities of life among the rank and file of believers. These realities are not only deemed worthy of study, but have come to be seen as the very stuff of renewal—as the deposit of faith, informed by the Spirit of the Lord. The expression of the people's faith—as subject to imperfection as that of any other group in the Church—is recognized as a true sign of the encounter between the Christian and his God. The temptation of the God-Magician on the popular plane is no less serious than that of the

God-Metaphysician on the philosophical.

Another factor which has influenced the change in attitude towards popular religion has been the emergence of a theology that is closer to human realities, more anthropological and less rationalist, essentialist and puritanical. The Christian people do not demean the faith when they live by it any more than a theologian when he speculates on it; but both stand to lose if they ignore or scorn each other, or claim excessive importance for themselves. The search for a mid-point between the two is what is making possible a true and proper assessment of popular religion.

Another element in the new situation has been the crisis undergone by an erudite pastoral ministry, built on patterns of life and worship proposed 'from above'. The extent to which this pastoral outlook has ignored the expressions of popular faith is the extent to which it has become a prey to its own religious puritanism.

The current interest in popular religion also owes something to the last and much discussed Synod of Bishops, which concentrated on evangelization and reflected the pastoral concerns of the Latin American Churches. Yet another element in the picture has been the general rehabilitation of popular culture and of its human and festive expressions in the face of the rationalism and secularism of a technological society.

The new attitude has also touched off a search for fresh hermeneutical guidelines with which to probe the human depths from which this type of religion springs, and assess its worth as an expression of the faith.[2]

SOCIOLOGICAL RESEARCH

It is against this background that we must see the sociological research that has been conducted into popular religious behaviour in Spain, for this frame of reference has influenced both the collection of empirical data and its subsequent interpretation. What is undeniable is that sociology and pastoral concern have met. There is hardly a diocese or church group (parish, sodality, apostolic association, and so on) which has not been subjected to socio-religious tests. On the other hand, there has also been suspicion from some sectors which fear for the survival of the supernatural and the doctrinal if empirical studies are brought to the fore.

During its first phase, sociological research was mostly factual and a tool of pastoral planning. It focussed mainly on observance, assessing the people's religion in relation to 'official' patterns without reference to anything that could be readily identified as 'popular culture'. The idea was to find out the extent to which the people had assimilated official religious expressions, not to look into their own. This first phase resulted in the books of D. Duocastella and J. M. Vázquez, published in 1967.[3]

But once its usefulness in the development of a keen pastoral response was acknowledged, the sober truth came to occupy a more prominent place in sociological research and the second stage dawned. Christian people and their religion ceased to be the mere target of such investigations; they themselves began to interpret the facts of their lives in the light of the faith, and to share in the renewal. The data obtained were not brought out in the typical scholarly books which are themselves proof against popular participation, but were turned into working documents for the benefit of small groups of individuals from all walks of life. The preliminary documents for the Joint Assembly of Bishops and Priests, as well as the sociological studies drafted in advance of the Diocesan Synod of Seville (1970–71) were of this type. Of late these sociological findings have been applied to the search for new pastoral insights and have also found a place for themselves in systematic formation (for instance, the projects undertaken in the Canary Islands, Albacete and Santander).

A more anthropological and phenomenological approach to the question has been typical of authors like Orensanz, Maldonado, Mateos and Martín Velasco, whose interest lies not so much in the empirical as in the hermeneutical, theological and pastoral aspects of this work.

SOME TRAITS OF SPANISH POPULAR RELIGION

We shall now note some of the salient traits of Spanish popular religion as brought to light by these socio-religious probes and interpreted by theologians and pastoral experts. Although such study is more properly concerned with individual and collective expressions of the transcendent, we shall mention a few facts about certain moral values and beliefs which are closely connected with it.

The belief in God which is the foundation of such religious expressions is almost universally accepted in popular circles (only three to five per cent doubt or deny it). But a substantial group (fifteen to twenty per cent) think of the Deity as something utterly transcendent, remote from the world and not exactly personal. The rest favour the image of the judge (forty per cent) or the father (forty per cent) when they think of God. Those who accept a personal God consider Christ His Son.

The Church is seen more as a beneficent and teaching institution providing religious services than as a Christian community, and much more domineering than spontaneous. To be a good Christian does not imply being a good 'observant'.

Between fifteen and twenty per cent do not believe in the resurrection, much less in hell (twenty-five per cent). This disbelief is however compatible with participation in religious acts at certain times of the year or on special occasions in private life.

Where *morals* are concerned popular religion is characterized by its insistence on probity and justice. Family ties bind strictly, although divorce on grounds of incompatibility is accepted by a growing number of people and there is toleration of premarital sex.

Popular *recourse to the sacraments* remains relatively constant as regards baptism, first communions and matrimony. Extreme unction has depended more on the initiative of the parish priest than the demand of the faithful; if a person is seriously ill the priest will normally be allowed in the house. Obsequies have great popular flavour, and the dead are usually accorded funeral rites. In Galicia especially the cult of the dead is widespread and intense.

Blessings and other *sacramentals* have lost much of their traditional popularity. Only one third of the population remains faithful to them while more than half openly rejects such time-honoured religious practices. The same holds true of the cult of the saints and its attendant expressions. The saints and their lore are an intimate part of popular religion, a much favoured stepping-stone in bridging the distance to God. In their midst but in a privileged place there stands the Mother of God, who is honoured in many shrines and who has inspired numerous pious customs, colourful and widely different in nature.

Processions—especially in Holy Week—still survive on a local plane and are even regaining acceptance in semi-rural districts. Processional brotherhoods and guilds still attract many, even the young. Certain pilgrimages can also be a mixture of local colour, culture and religion. Corpus Christi processions on the other hand have lost much ground in urban centres while those in commemoration of the saints or linked to other liturgical festivities have almost disappeared.

Religious fiestas in honour of local patron saints have become extremely secularized and their programmes now barely include any of the old, routine religious acts. The conflict between the religious and the profane has become an almost invariable feature of this type of celebration.

As regards other events on the liturgical calendar, it is well to note that in Spain a good number of major religious feasts are national holidays (January 1, St Joseph's on March 19, Holy Thursday and Good Friday, the Ascension, Corpus Christi, St James's, the Feast of Saints Peter and Paul, the Assumption, the Feast of our Lady of the

Pillar, All Saints Day, Christmas . . . and the feast days of local patron saints). Many of these are observed as secular holidays without much reference to their traditional religious content.

Certain *devotions* are still in existence (novenas, First Fridays, Month of May devotions) but their supporters are fewer every day in spite of the efforts of certain conservative movements, more bent on proffering traditional certainties than on marching alongside the Church towards the crossroads discerned by the Council.

THE CHANGING PICTURE AND THE REASONS BEHIND IT

In Spain popular religion has evolved under the influence of powerful new factors in the life of Christians. Some of these have arisen from the social change that has overtaken the nation, others from the pastoral outlook of the new generation of priests.

Social change has had its most serious effects on the structure of those communities who are the bearers of traditional religious values. Its two main characteristics have been geographical mobility—with great migrations within the country and across its boundaries—and the coming of the mass media.

Migrations have clearly disrupted the fibre of the community, weakening the social nexus which underlies its religious life; the anonymity engendered by rapid urbanization has also destroyed this communal support. On the other hand, the mass media's sudden revelation of alternative lifestyles, of pluralistic secular and religious outlooks, has shattered the proofs of a world inevitably related to God and to the Christian faith. Technology, for its part, has solved certain problems formerly brought before God in collective prayer (rogation days, prayers for rain, and so on).

A second set of factors are the result of *pastoral* praxis. The emphasis on witness and on the prophetic character of Christian life has left worship and the social expressions of the faith in the lurch. It is not uncommon for a parish priest to balk at the celebration of popular rites alleging the primacy of the personal in matters of faith, or pointing to the contradiction between the private witness of the participants and their presence at a religious act. Some of the clergy have even gone so far so to bask, to a certain extent, in the antithesis between faith and religion: the very thought of the transcendent or appeal to divine providence in the face of human problems is enough to rouse suspicion of an alienating, escapist religion.

To sum up, the new and earnest reappraisal of popular religion springs from a longing for certain values which have been relinquished or ignored by contemporary culture and more specifically by the

Church of our times. The loss of the festive element in liturgical celebrations, the use of a stark symbolism that has virtually nothing to say to the people's sensibilities, the younger generation's search for fresh religious expressions within a new popular culture, the urge to be done with the conventional ways of ancient institutions, the renaissance of the mystic and the imaginary; in short, a widespread awareness that the popular must be reassessed and readmitted as an active component of the Church's renewal, is what lies at the bottom of current interest in the topic.

This paper has deliberately avoided mention of the maudlin and extravagant side of some popular religious expressions. It has posited popular religion in its best and purest sense as the outpouring of the Christian people, worthy of all respect in theological speculation, sociological study and pastoral praxis.

Translated by T. F. Buons

Notes

1. The most important books are: *El Catolicismo Popular en el Sur de España* (a working document drafted by the bishops of the southern region) (Madrid, 1975), 47 pp.; L. Maldonado, *Religiosidad popular, nostalgia de lo mágico* (Madrid, 1975), 365 pp.; A. L. Orensanz, *Religiosidad Popular Española 1940–1965* (Madrid, 1974); the journals that have devoted special issues to the theme are *Pastoral Misionera,* January-February 1975; *Proyección,* May-June 1975 and *Phase* 89, 1975.

2. In the work in reference L. Maldonado explores the hermeneutical guidelines inherent in the symbolic, the magic, the imaginary, the mystic, the festive, the farcical, theatrical, communal and political. His erudition on these subjects and the depths of his insights make this a key work in the study of popular religion.

3. R. Duocastella, J. Marcos, J. M. Díaz Mozaz, *Análisis Sociológico del catolicismo español* (Barcelona, 1967). J. M. Vásquez, *Realidades Socio-religiosas de España* (Madrid, 1967).

David Power

Cultural Encounter and
Religious Expression

APART from the time of its beginnings in Israel, Christianity has always been a faith which came from outside the cultural setting of the place where it was preached. It has always arrived in an alien cultural dress, and so has always been faced with the problem of a fusion of cultures. How far evangelization needs to affect the cultural modes of the evangelized is an ever-recurring question. In this article, the intention is to examine the implications of this problem, in the interest of new developments. Can we discern, in its most basic forms, the influence which faith has on cultural expression? On the other hand, can we see how faith may be stifled by the failure to meet the cultural problem?

CULTURE

Definitions and descriptions of culture are often based on the image of a self-contained society. There is harmony, organic unity, unified vision. A person does not have to look too far to find his values. They are given in the rites, institutions, traditions and myths of his people. His life partakes of a cosmic force: along with his tribe, he is at the centre of the universe and the still turning-point of time.

Like Augustine on time, we know what culture is but cannot define it accurately. Loosely speaking, we can say that it includes economic, political and religious systems. It is whatever is expressed in traditions, beliefs, customs, institutions, arts and artifacts, symbols, myths and rites. Its core is the values and the meaning on which human life, individual and collective, is based. The idyllic picture of culture is that it represents a unified whole. Of religion within such a pattern, it would be said that it harmonizes with all else, is interwoven with it, and somehow indicates that life is sacred.

Whatever the truth of such a description, there is hardly a single example in the world today of a society and a culture which has not entered into contact and conflict with other cultures. Patterns have been unwoven, so that there are no holy centres from which a group derives undisputed value and meaning. Meeting the economic and political crises of the day may mean discounting religion as a vital factor in the harmonious development of society. Men are trying to live peacefully together, despite rather fundamental differences on questions of life and death. Nonetheless, those who live by faith remain convinced that to them at least it should be the source and focal point of meaning in life. Moreover, societies which have been religious in their foundations do not expel all semblance thereof too lightly from their fabric, and some religious practice can remain side by side with very secular attitudes.

PARADIGMS

As paradigms of the place which religion has in current cultural experiences, we can take three examples as a starting-point for reflection. These are messianism in Africa, the 'religiosidad popular' of Latin America, and the religious practices of the populace of the city of Rome.

Messianism in Africa[1]

Observers do not all agree on the significance and force of messianism in African countries and churches. It is some blending of beliefs and traditions taken from traditional religions and from an imported Christianity: imported, that is, in the garb that it had acquired through long centuries of dwelling in Europe. Messianism is the expression and creation of (or for) the less sophisticated members of peoples whose life-structures have been fragmented by the intrusion on their continent of the white races, bringing with them new economics, new politics, new family customs and new religions. Often enough, the religion was initially accepted along with the rest, but like the rest did not meet its promises of betterment. Neither the wholesale return to traditional religions, nor the wholesale adherence to western forms of Christianity, can remedy a rather disappointing situation. Messianism in its various shapes endeavours to integrate elements from the clashing cultures into a religious practice which spells hope. It is not a homogeneous phenomenon, its message of hope is not the same in all places and in all the emerging 'Churches', but its common point of interest is its attempt to give unity, wholeness and promise.

At this juncture in its history, African messianism has an apocalyptic sound. As is the wont of apocalyptic, it can draw people towards visions of millennium. It can be the promise of good things not to be sought for in politics and economics (where people cannot cope anyway), but which will be given by some saving hand to those whose resignation in face of hardships will bear its reward, or to those who practice the virtues of thrift and hard work, avoiding the vices born of despair and displacement. On the other hand, it can be a more positive force, which engenders an effort to achieve self-determination. Since it is apocalyptic, it will belittle the apparent might of invading forces and systems. It will teach that these are not necessary for salvation and improvement. It can convey a spirit which impels a people to do all that it can to shape out its own place on the earth. The more it draws on the people's own past and mythologies, the more it can convince them that out of their own heritage they can build up a future, not relying on a return to the past ways but in a truly creative spirit.

Whether this messianism is syncretistic or not, depends on how it weds the elements taken from different cultures, and on what kind of hope it gives. If its main purpose is to make daily life more bearable, it will probably be syncretistic in the worst sense of the term, for it will take from either religion whatever seem the best practices to satisfy particular needs. A Christian saint and an African charm may be a good combination in time of sickness. A miracle story from the gospels and some of the titles of Christ can go well with local legends to build up an ideal messianic figure, whose help is expected in times of hardship and in giving some immediate happiness in festivities, or in promising social position to the thrifty and abstemious.

The more, however, that it seeks to foster trust in the spirit that is within, the more likely it is to achieve a unified vision and expression. It can go beyond the stages of syncretism and forge a new mentality. The creative blending of past and future exacts this, whereas a limited concern with a daily present will be content with lesser gains, and prone to invoke whatever power is deemed attendant on the day's calamities. The unity which is achieved beyond syncretism is not one that emerges from a piecing together of cultural contents. It derives from attention to the dynamic thrust of symbols, and from a learning of the processes of story-telling and symbol-making. The people that can tell stories of their own death and rebirth can also live in hope, and in that hope create elements of a new order.

'Religiosidad popular' in Latin America[2]

The 'religiosidad popular' of Latin America springs from the twinning of a people's economic and political defeat with the impositions, and maybe the promises, of an invader's Christianity. The most severe criticism made of it, is that it engenders no hope, no authentic liberation. Blending together elements from African religions, Indian cults, and Spanish or Portuguese Christianity, it is the religion of an enslaved people, which leads too readily to submission and resignation. It provides a kind of infertile festivity, taking the mind off the more serious consequences of one's social position, or lack thereof. Even if it includes the Christian sacraments, it is not true Christianity, but the pabulum of a people whose own histories and values are ignored, or counted as dross. It is for a people without a real history, and its mortal sin is that it can give them none. Latin Americans are often ethnically the offspring of mixed racial groups, the sons and daughters of those who from the start were meant to serve. Colonials from Europe, who had no footing there, mixed with the Indians or the African slaves and produced progeny 'without father' and 'without name', whose sweat could serve to build the bricks of the dominant minority. What they learned about Christianity served to keep them in their place. At best, they were ensured eternal salvation if they kept the moral and religious laws.[3] From other religious systems, such people can find those factors which help them to survive each day. To invoke an African slave among one's ancestors may teach one to be resigned to one's lot. It may even foment a sterile hatred of the overlord. Could such an invocation ever become a vital force for freedom?

Religious Practice of Romans[4]

From data collected in 1969–70, a sociologist was led to express the opinion that whilst some ninety per cent of Rome's populace at some stage in their lives practiced the rites of the Catholic Church, only five per cent are authentically Catholic. While one may justifiably quibble over his interpretation of the data (sociologists not being infallible), it remains a fact that in Rome there is a religious practice which does not seem to express what the rites themselves intend, if they are taken in their historical purity. It is another case of the common man's religion (and he may be a millionaire industrialist as easily as a *barracche* dweller). In this case, however, it is not the result of a meeting between cultures. Rather, it is linked with a cultural development of changing values and visions, attendant on technological and social progress. The traditional rites of the Catholic religion do not seem to fit, and for many they matter little enough. Yet the practices continue, giving rise to a series of questions about the religious sense they express.

From these three paradigms, something emerges about the pattern of religious practice in the present time. In times past, religion was all-pervasive and at the heart of the matter. Sacred and profane were not separable, except in the sense that the profane was the unintegrated. A society's religion was at one with its cultural values and meanings. If you did not share them, you were a sect (as was the case of Christians in imperial Rome) and that meant living outside the social pale. All that has changed, and with the diversification of cultures has come a disruption of religious belief and practice. In this new state of affairs, the position of religion is variable. It may be rather on the fringe of what is happening. It may be put to use to reconcile people to the fact that development has passed them by, without giving them a share in its benefits. It may, however, also seek new forms which allow it to insert its presence at the heart of where things are going. It must then be asked whether there are criteria available to permit a critique of what occurs.

A CHRISTIAN'S CRITIQUE OF RELIGIOUS EXPRESSION

The key question in this critique is the following: is the core of Christianity content and form, or is it a particular dynamics of religious experience? To put this in other words: is it doctrine and ritual, or is it a dynamics of faith, which structures the human experience of the transcendent?

If the answer to this query favours content and form, then the task of evangelization is that of adaptation and acculturation (or incarnation). To use the second of these terms is considered more progressive than to use the former, because it allows more readily for internal growth, and reduces in number the tenets of doctrine and the forms of ritual considered essential. It makes more place for dialogue with other religious traditions. However, its implications have hardly been worked out as yet, particularly in regard to the relation between content and dynamics.

If the view taken of Christianity is that it is a dynamics of religious meaning, then we must have principles of action to guide its expression and its relation to other religions and cultures.

A first principle is that religion is consummated in faith, and that faith grounds religion when it is authentic.[5] As Bernard Lonergan says, faith is the knowledge which is born of love, of being in love in an unrestricted fashion. It is a dynamic state of being, a movement towards self-transcendence and towards communion in spirit. In more biblical terms, it is the Spirit of God within man, the Spirit speaking to our spirit, seeking to create a communion in love, transcending divisions, and finding ultimate oneness in the mystery which abides in all things: 'Religious experience spontaneously manifests itself in changed attitudes, in the harvest of the Spirit that is love, joy, peace, kindness, goodness, fidelity, gentleness and self-control. But it is also concerned with its basis and focus in the *mysterium fascinans et tremendum*'.[6] It will not develop unless given expression, and the expression will be culturally manifold. It may also be stultifying, to the extent that it arises from inauthentic experience, and one of the most stultifying factors is to allow preoccupation with content and form outride dynamics and inner consciousness.

In Christian terms, what is to be lived is the father-son relationship, for which Christ is paradigmatic. It is a relationship which exists only in the Spirit, and finds its fulfilment in the Spirit. As Paul Ricoeur comments:

Far from being easy to address God as Father, by looking into an archaic past, such address is rare, difficult and audacious, because it is prophetic. It is turned to the future and to accomplishment, rather than to beginnings. It does not look backward to a great ancestor, but forward in the direction of a new intimacy, modelled on the knowledge of the son. In Paul's exegesis, it is because the Spirit testifies to our sonship (Rom 8.16) that we can cry, Abba, Father. Far then from being a hostile and distant transcendence, the religion of the father is a fatherhood which exists because there is sonship, and there is sonship because there is communion in the spirit.[7]

This dynamics is not maintained without inner freedom. The spirit of servitude tempts us to adopt ossifying formulations, with which to rest content and secure, keeping the distance between God and man which protects from yielding to him in oneness of spirit. To religious expression, Christian faith can contribute the necessary freedom.

When it is emphasised that faith is a dynamics, the second important principle to be kept in mind is what might be called 'the intention of truth' in symbolic expression.[8] In symbols and their variant use, peoples express their quest for meaning. They indicate how man experiences life and what sense he makes of it.

This is a field in which the meaning of terms is not fixed. To avoid confusion, let us try to make some matters clear on how reality is perceived and truth appropriated.

For some, whose world is only that of feelings, reality is identified with images and sense perceptions. It is in that world that they live and move and have their being. To be responsible, to truly love, to know the mystery of life, they must needs go beyond such a world, recognize the need to transcend the world of sense, to conform feeling to reality and not vice versa. The artist and the philosopher are thought to have an important part in culture, because they can break the world of feelings and challenge to new perceptions of reality.

The 'sophisticated' westerner tries to come to grips with these different worlds by making distinctions. There is the primitive world, in which people live completely by feeling, identify the worldy and the other-worldly with their myths. Then there is the more advanced world, in which the artists have their part, since with literary and other skills they challenge perception and invite to new projects. Then there is the world of the philosopher, who makes clear the distinction between sense and thought, feelings and love, subjective and objective, experienced and unexperienced, immediate and mediated.

In effect, cultures which are built on mythologies, symbols, customs, traditions, rituals, may be more differentiated than the western observer is inclined to think. They may have (in some cases certainly do have) their own ways to shock and challenge reality sense. Consciousness of the 'known unknown' and of the need to transcend the self to enter into it, is awakened by the interplay of myths, symbols, parables, metaphors, narratives, images and rites. There are more ways than the philosophical to invite to interiority. Indeed, as we have come to acknowledge, the interplay of symbols is necessary for this, since feelings must be shocked and invited if thought and decision are to be set free. Language studies show more and more how this is done. Some application is made to the study of the Bible, particularly in regard to myth, narrative and parable.[9] In the work of evangelization and faith-insertion in other cultures, their own language devices have to be put to use.

Paul Ricoeur gives us some paradigms for a 'discernment of myths'.[10] In his study of the myths of evil, his stance was not that of a substitution of one myth for the rest, but an appropriation of all myths within the perspective and dynamic of one, which is allowed to dominate because it offers greater freedom to man's creative spirit, and greater hope in the pursuit of good:

> By putting all other myths into perspective with relation to a dominant myth (i.e., the Adamic), we bring into light a circularity among the myths and we make possible the substitution of a dynamics for a statics of the myths; in place of a static view of myths regarded as having equal rights, the dynamic view makes manifest the

struggle among the myths. The appropriation of the struggle among the myths is itself a struggle for appropriation.[11]

The crucial question for Christianity's religious expression is whence it derives its power to free man, or to free the spirit that is at work in man. If this dynamics can be discovered, then it can be introduced into any culture or religion. Of its very nature, it allows for creative development of language, a dynamics of symbols, within culture.

Perhaps Italo Mancini has found a happy expression of the dynamics of Christian faith, when he says that Christianity always preaches *kairos, doxa* and *eschaton,* and that it necessarily lives a spiral whereby it takes form, contests all forms, and prefigures new forms.[12] The cycle, or spiral, of forms inevitably follows within a vision of the time of salvation which allows for the praise of God and gives rise to hope for the future.

The proclamation of *kairos* turns every moment into the 'still turning-point of time', makes of it a moment in eternity in which the God of love is encountered. The sense of *kairos* is well expressed by David Tracy, when he says that 'the proclamatory sayings of Jesus do not provide us time-plans for the kingdom as future, as past, or as present. Rather . . . these sayings actually bestow on us the event of an authentic time: time as the e-vent, the happening, for the disclosure of God's gracious and trustworthy action to happen now'.[13]

This sense of salvific time leads to a particular way of viewing and narrating history. The Christian witness combats any particularism which selects one people in preference to another. It announces God as a God whose saving Spirit blows where he wills. Its witness is to this Spirit, this love of God, at work in all time, in all history, and in any particular history. The past of a people is to be symbolically interpreted in keeping with this vision. The effort must be to give this interpretation not from without, but from within, its own memory and symbolic traditions. Without such a memory of the past, which automatically coincides with a hope for the future, the present will always appear as a moment to be survived, instead of as a point of God's promise and covenant.

Awareness of 'God's gracious and trustworthy action' fosters an attitude of praise. Praise is the antidote to the magical tendencies inherent in any religious system, and it is the only adequate way in which God may be invoked as Father. Too facile a tendency to call God 'Father' has been the bane of Christianity and one of the major obstacles to true evangelization. The missionary Church is tempted to pick out points in non-Christian traditions whereby to illustrate, or allegorize, a fatherhood which is related to creation, origin and beneficence. In effect, this encourages a superstitious and inert dependence, and a magical approach to rite. The paternity we proclaim of God is more truly related to alliance, promise and choice. It exacts a fidelity similar to that between spouses, and one which promises freedom to the adopted children. An impoverishment and self-emptying is required if his power is to be known. This is an attitude in face of the mysteriousness of God's love, such as is found in Job, or in the just man of wisdom literature who in his suffering and though reviled by men keeps his trust in God. The enigma of this relationship 'makes sense' only in Jesus' invocation of God as his 'Abba'. This invocation could not be made if there were no recognition that God has given his Spirit to his Son, and that the son-father relationship is grounded in this alliance in the Spirit.[14]

An appropriation of the trajectory of the Judeo-Christian revelation may well serve as a preparation for the man who seeks ways in which to express the Christian *doxa* in non-Semitic and non-Mediterranean cultures. He will have learned thereby how far Judaism is a purification of other religions, and how far Jesus wished to proclaim what would have been an authentic Judaism, one purified of many of its embolisms. Ricoeur's studies of symbol and myth show how far the 'dilemma of God' or the 'enigma of the transcendent' were inherited by the Jewish people from non-Jewish mythologies and traditions. It is an encounter with the prophetic announcement of *kairos* that religious traditions are purified and develop, and eventually come to a point where God can be invoked and praised as Father.

Christian evangelization has often been too preoccupied with Christianity's institutional elements. This is an obstacle to a liturgy of praise and a ritual which can find a place in other cultures. Whatever about flexibility in word and catechesis, the Church has shown very little flexibility in recent centuries in sacramental worship, least of all in the Eucharist. Even today, the Curia feels obliged to authenticate the translation of the words of consecration into Xhosa and Tagalog. But how do we know that such a translation conveys anything of the dynamics of the relationship between God and Christ, or between Christ and those whom he loved on the Father's account, even to the shedding of his blood?

The creed and the eucharistic prayer proclaim and praise, in the first place, the God of creation. This has little to do with the 'ex nihilo sui et subiecti' of scholastic theology. It has much to do with the cosmogonies taken up by the prophetic tradition in ages past, and interpreted and appropriated from the stance of the Adamic or Pentateuchal variation of these myths. The creed and eucharistic prayer proclaim that Jesus Christ gave his life in sacrifice for the many. This has little to do with the reverence to God's honour about which the Tridentine Fathers were so preoccupied. It has much to do with the covenant treaties that Abraham found necessary in portioning out the land for his flocks and for those of his rival herdsmen, with the human sacrifices whereby Israel and her neighbours sought to enter into the cycle of time, with the blood wherewith fearful man sought to wash away his sins and guilt—and with the love which traced a path through the labyrinth of fear, guilt, jealousy, and scandal.

He who wishes to proclaim God's praise among a people must needs take on the ways in which it has sought to wrestle with the harshness of the earth, the enigma of life, the fear of death and oblivion, the constant struggle for power and possession which destroys community. How can the people be freed? How can their stories be told and retold, so as to weave a path of freedom and hope through the maze of agony, fear and superstition? How can the truth that is in these stories and customs be liberated and set into the light of day? How may God be praised in authentic words, rather than in the babblings of the enslaving language of another culture's institutional preoccupations?

The time of salvation and praise is a future-filled, hopeful anticipation of life. Persuaded of the life in the Spirit, a people can live in hope. It can work towards that hope, for the 'Spirit speaks to our spirit', and is the ground of liberation.

The critique of forms, the taking-on of new forms, a critique of these same when they in turn begin to ossify, a constant prefiguring and pretasting of new forms, is a necessary part of the spiral of saving presence, praise and hope. It is the work of free spirits. The tendency of a religious system, and this is no less true of Christianity than of other religions, can be to suppress the creative spirit. He is a threat to ground gained, and so repudiated. Fortunately, it can be a redemptive suffering for others, provided that his story is told and appropriated.

It is one of the theses of Joseph Campbell in his work *The Masks of God,* and especially in the volume *Creative Mythology*,[15] that in the western world the creative spirit works only outside organized Christendom. Campbell points to a path going from the legends of the Grail and similar literature to recent writers such as Joyce and Mann. Along this path, creative individuals have travelled in a desire to be free from the 'anticipated death' of traditional mythologies and established formulas. His criticism may be exaggerated, but has undoubtedly its moment of truth. All too often, in the story of Christendom, individuals, on the pain of death or ex-communication, have been required to submit to the mass or to the structure. But the true 'mythology' of Christian faith offers solidarity in the paradox of the lonely quest of the individual, in the wilderness experience of a taking-on of Christ's sonship. There has to be a dissociation from much that is established, if truth is to be pursued.

There is a Christian ideal which says that the ecclesial community is a fellowship of free spirits, free that is in the Spirit. The desire to allow for a Christianity that is of the masses works against this, for expression begins to succumb to the formalism which satisfies masses unprovoked to thought or awakened consciousness. However, the symbol of the small remnant within the cultural tradition is part of the dynamic of the Judeo-Christian faith. Paradoxically, it is not a small remnant which seeks to isolate itself. Like Christ, it seeks to be 'for the many'. It knows the tendency to formalism and ritualism, but does not despair, because it has the Spirit. It is patient enough to know that salvation is a history, and that a dialectic of forms is necessary. It is senseless to talk of a dialectic, unless allowance is made for the words which people use to express their actual selves. People must be allowed to sing the songs they wish to sing, and the small remnant does not baulk at that. But it will make its own contribution by way of prophetic song, a song which frees and holds out future promise, which provokes and challenges, even if it risks also angering and disturbing.

SUMMARY AND CONCLUSION

Behind much of the malaise over prevailing forms of 'popular religiosity' is the failure to resolve questions of faith-expression when cultures meet. On the one hand, the Christian from a 'foreign' culture fails to perceive the intention of truth in the strivings of other religions or traditions. On the other, any religious expression, including that of Christianity, is constantly subject to the temptation to identify reality and faith with conceptual content and linguistic form. Either mistake blocks the development of new ways of saying, and leaves a strange mingling of bodies, foreign to one another.

Few myths, customs or rites need be rejected out of hand, without more ado. Faith allows a Christian to be free in regard to his own culture, and to invite his partner in dialogue to be similarly free in his habitat. Myths and histories and rites can be 'played with' in creative freedom, so that their feeling for man's life and its meaning is unearthed and their enslaving demon expelled, giving rebirth to the hope of which they bear the seed and the promise.

Today, culture and religion are in foment, the component 'religion' apparently less relevant. The answer is not a purely secular mentality, a concentration on man's own realm to the exclusion of the gods. If we secularize man's problems and meanings completely, 'God need no longer be counted upon to solve problems in the world; the problems—at the level at which divine intervention would avail—have been dissolved'.[16] If Christian proclamation and prayer 'attends first, foremost and exclusively to what the given is given *to*, it winds up with nothing *given* to. More especially, it does not allow the given to identify the world and its decisive strifes, to interrogate the world and the world's self-analysis, and to establish that world in which man is to be housed in fulfillment'.[17]

Enslaved to the present, in disjunction from past and future, tied down to forms of prayer and rite intended to obtain divine beneficence, assuring only the future of afterlife to undo the hardships of the present, religion is both enslaved and enslaving. Suffuse it with the Christian Gospel of *kairos, doxa* and *eschaton*, and it becomes a fomenting presence in any culture, one which sets free in the power of the Spirit, so that man may house the world to his own peace and to the glory of God.

Notes

1. See D. B. Barrett, *Schism and Renewal in Africa* (Oxford, 1968); L.-V. Thomas and R. Luneau, *La Terre Africaine et Ses Religions* (Paris, 1975), pp. 322–7.

2. For a bibliography and a critique, see José Miguez Bonino, 'Popular Piety in Latin America', *Concilium 6,* 10 (June, 1974), pp. 148–57. For an evaluation, see Celam, *Catequesis latinoamericana,* Ano VI, n. 2 (1974), PR 94–9.

3. On missionary catechesis in early times, see J. Specker, *Der Missionsmethode in Spanisch-Amerika im 16. Jahrhundert* (Fribourg, Switzerland, 1953), pp. 94–135; W. Reinhard, *The Evangelization of Brazil under the Jesuits (1549–1568),* Dissertatio ad Lauream, PUG (Rome, 1969), pp. 285–300.

4. E. Pin, *La Religiosità dei Romani* (Bologna, 1975).

5. Cf. B. Lonergan, *Method in Theology* (London, 1972), pp. 101–19.

6. *Op. cit.,* p. 108.

7. P. Ricoeur, 'La Paternité: Du Fantasme au Symbole', in *Le Conflit des Interprétations* (Paris, 1969), p. 480.

8. Cf. G. Barden, 'The Intention of Truth in Mythic Consciousness', in P. McShane (ed.), *Language, Truth and Meaning* (Dublin, 1972), pp. 4–32.

9. For a summary and bibliography of such attempts, cf. D. Tracy, *Blessed Rage for Order* (New York, 1975), pp. 120–45.

10. P. Ricoeur, *La Symbolique du Mal* (Paris, 1960), pp. 285–321.

11. *Ibid.,* p. 288; Engl. trans., *The Symbolism of Evil* (Boston, 1967), p. 309.

12. I. Mancini, 'Cultura cristiana: specificità e senso', in *Christianesimo e Cultura: Atti del XLVI corso di aggironamento culturale dell'università cattolica: Loreto, 21-26 settembre 1975* (Milan, 1975), pp. 36–57.

13. *Op. cit.*, p. 134.

14. Cf. P. Ricoeur, 'La paternité', *loc. cit.*

15. J. Campbell, *The Masks of God: Creative Mythology* (New York, 1968).

16. R. Hart, *Unfinished Man and the Imagination* (New York, 1968), p. 39.

17. *Ibid.*

Contributors

ANSCAR CHUPUNGCO, O.S.B., is Professor of the History of Liturgy and Liturgical Adaptation at the Pontifical Institute in Rome and Professor of Pastoral Liturgy at the Maryhill School of Theology, Rizal, Philippines. He has published *Misa ng Bayang Pilipino*—a study of liturgical indigenization (Quezon City, 1975).

IRENEE-HENRI DALMAIS, O.P., is Professor of Oriental Liturgy at the Institut Supérieur de Liturgie, Paris; his publications include *Initiation à la Liturgie* (Paris, 1958), *Saints et Sanctuaires d'Orient* (Paris, 1968) and (with others) *Shalom: Chrétiens à l'écoute des grandes religions* (Paris, 1972).

LESLIE DESMANGLES was born in Haiti and is Assistant Professor of Religion at DePaul University, Chicago. He has conducted field research into Rastafarian and other cults in Jamaica and into Vodun in Haiti. His doctoral dissertation was on the symbiosis of Catholic saints and Vodun deities.

JEAN-MARC ELA was born in Ebolowa, Cameroon, and ordained priest in 1964. His doctoral theses was on divine transcendence and human existence according to Luther. He has published various articles on pastoral theology and African affairs. He has been a missionary among the Cameroon highlanders since 1971.

VIRGIL ELIZONDO was born in San Antonio, Texas, and has been President of the Mexican American Cultural Centre in San Antonio since 1971. Among his publications are *A Search for Meaning in Life and Death* (Manila, 1971) and *Christianity and Culture* (Huntington, 1975).

JACQUES FONTAINE was born in Paris in 1922. He has represented the University of Caen at international meetings and conferences. He is a member of various international bodies and notably of the

Scientific Council of the Institut des Hautes Etudes Hispaniques, Madrid, and a foreign corresponding member of the Real Academia de la Historia, Madrid. Among his publications are *Isidore de Seville et la culture classique dans l'Espagne wisigothique* (Paris, 1959) and *La littérature latine chrétienne* (Paris, 1970).

VICENT JOSEP SASTRE GARCIA, S.J., was born in Valencia in 1931, and was Director of the survey on the Spanish clergy undertaken for the joint assembly of Spanish bishops and priests. He is now Technical Director of the Department of Sociology of the Spanish Hierarchy and of the Sociological Research Seminar of the University of Comillas, and Professor of Sociology in the Department of Philosophy at Comillas.

JOAN LLOPIS was born in Barcelona in 1932. He was Professor of Liturgy at the University of Salamanca and at the Barcelona School of Theology. Among his publications are *Itinerari liturgic* (Barcelona, 1968) and *El entierro cristiano* (Madrid, 1972).

DAVID POWER, O.M.I., was born in Ireland in 1932 and ordained priest in 1956. He is now Professor of Sacramental Theology and Liturgy at the Gregorian University, Rome. Among his publications are *Ministers of Christ and his Church* (London, 1969) and *Christian Priest: Elder and Prophet* (London, 1973).

KLEMENS RICHTER was born in Leipzig in 1940. He is Reader in Liturgy in Münster. Among his publications are *Die kirchliche Trauung* (Freiburg, 1976) and *Die Ordination des Bischofs von Rom* (Münster, 1976).

HERMAN SCHMIDT, S.J., was born in 1912 in Roermond, the Netherlands. He is Professor of Liturgy at the Gregorian University, Rome, and at the St Anselm Institute of Liturgy, Rome. His publications include *Liturgie et langue vulgaire* (Paris, 1950) and *Wie betet der heutige Mensch* (Freiburg, 1972).